What they're saying .

The GUS CHRONICLES

Every child and youth care worker needs to step into the thoughts of youth at risk in order to understand why they act like they do. Charlie Appelstein uses his broad experiences in the field – and his considerable creative writing skills – to give voice to a fictional youth-in-care. By drawing us into his world-view, Gus gives the reader fresh perspectives on what it might be like to live in one of these places we adults call treatment centers. This book will take its place in the training literature along with the genre such as Mark Krueger's novels on child care work. Textbooks just can't say it like Gus does.

Larry Brendtro
President
Reclaiming Children and Youth

Deciding to use **The GUS CHRONICLES** *as the first reading assignment to supplement the text in my Introduction to Psychology course this Fall is the best decision I could have made. As it happens,* **The GUS CHRONICLES** *is the perfect way to introduce some of the major terms and concepts, as well as serious themes and theories of psychology. After working with Gus, students become enthusiastic and gained confidence in their ability to analyze and apply the psychology concepts raised in Gus to other contexts. Gus is highly appropriate in that it appeals to a wide range of diverse student learning styles and levels. I am very glad that I decided to adopt Gus and strongly recommend it as a motivational resource to supplement any psychology text.*

Claire Cummings, Ph.D., Psychology Instructor
Department of Arts and Sciences,
Newbury College, Brookline, MA

... Charlie Appelstein has portrayed Gus as a thoroughly believable account of an abused and troubled youth. Gus's recollections of his first day in residential care were so chillingly similar to mine that I quickly forgot Gus was not real.

John R. Seita, Ph.D., Program Director,
Kellogg Youth Initiative Partnerships, Marshall, MI

The
GUS CHRONICLES

Reflections From An Abused Kid

About: Sexual & Physical Abuse,
Residential Treatment, Foster Care,
Family Unification, and Much More

Charles D. Appelstein, M.S.W.
(and Gus E. Studelmeyer)

Sixth Edition

Published by Appelstein Professional Services
Salem, New Hampshire

THE GUS CHRONICLES

REFLECTIONS FROM AN ABUSED KID

Library of Congress Catalog Card Number 95-60468

Copies of this book may be purchased by order form located on the back page.

Appelstein Professional Services provides training, consultation, and literature to programs, schools, and parent associations nationwide that seek support in understanding and responding to the challenging behavior of children and youth. For more information, visit our website: www.charliea.com or contact us at: charliea@attbi.com.

ISBN-0-9719640-0-9

Preface

A good story can be more powerful than experience, for it lures us into the inner world of persons we otherwise would not have had the opportunity to know. When I picked up *The Gus Chronicles*, I was transported back to the time I served as a counselor in a summer camp for troubled Detroit kids who acted like Gus. My co-workers and I were young, idealistic and armed with some baccalaureate behavioral theory – but little practice wisdom. Without the script of these youths' secret battle plan, we could not decode their hostile behavior, so we were whipped around. Veteran adult-fighters, they responded to our friendly gestures with x-rated words and war-like acts. In an impressive show of reverse behavior modification, the "campers" would transform the "counselors." They sucked us into conflict cycles and counter aggression. If only we had been able to read a book like *The Gus Chronicles*, then perhaps we could have deciphered the hurt that was buried beneath the hate. This book is for any person who wants deeply to understand and help angry, adult wary youth. Unless we have personally experienced severe abuse, we cannot imagine how deep the wounds can be. In *The Gus Chronicles*, we see how much courage it takes to learn to trust again, and how hard adults must work to be worthy of that trust.

Larry Brendtro
President
Reclaiming Children and Youth

To the memory of my father, Edward Appelstein.
A dad Gus should have had.

And to Floyd Alwon, Ed.D., Director of the Walker-Trieschman Center, a division of the Child Welfare League of America:

Thank you for your courage and unyielding support in bringing Gus to print. You have been a remarkable advocate for at-risk kids. I treasure the work we have done together and value our friendship.

Table of Contents

Introduction

My name is Gus E. Studelmeyer. I'm a fictitious teenage character. I think that stinks! How would you like to live inside of a damn book? Me, I want to live. I want to taste things. I want to have sex!

I was created sometime during 1990. The author got this wonderful inspiration one night and.....voila.......Gus E. Studelmeyer, at your service.

I am your "almost" typical abused, emotionally disturbed adolescent, complete with zits and red hair, living in a residential treatment center.

The author created me and then asked that I write an essay about life in residential treatment. He thought it would be cool for people to get a look at residential treatment from an abused kid's perspective. At first, I turned him down. I didn't like the fact that he made me pudgy with red hair and zits. But being fictititious made me what one might call a weak negotiator. So I wrote the darn essay and disappeared. Three months go by and—BANG—the dude shows up again asking me to write a follow-up essay. This time he wants me to write about tantrums and physical restraint. "Wow, that'll be fun."

So, I write the physical restraint story and wait to see what will happen next?

"WRITE A BOOK...ARE YOU CRAZY? Who has the energy to write a friggin' book? The only Page this guy is interested in has two legs and a nice pair of you-know-whats!"

Again, it was an offer I could not refuse. Two years later, I dotted the last "i" of chapter ten and here you have it. Now that it's written, I can see it was

3

worth the effort.

One more thing about me that's important to mention. As you will see in the first chapter, the author has endowed me with quite a brain. I'm able to conceptualize things and use vocabulary light years ahead of my peers. Certainly, having such exceptional intellect is not typical of abused kids living in residential treatment. For that matter, it's not typical of most thirteen year-olds living anywhere. The reason, I am told, for having such gifts centers on purpose.

Gus E. Studelmeyer, yours truly, was created for the purpose of helping adults, and in particular, child care professionals, better understand and empathize with abused children living in residential care. The author thought hearing about this stuff from a kid's perspective would make it more interesting and meaningful. Yet, although my intellect and vocabulary are not typical, I believe the *feelings* I express throughout this book are indeed typical of abused kids.

Speaking of feelings, let me address a somewhat sensitive issue. To truly express my feelings as an abused kid living behind the walls of residential treatment, I sometimes, throughout the course of this book, use some rather naughty expletive deleteds. Hey, angry, abused kids swear. There ain't no friggin' way around it. (I controlled myself that time.) Hopefully, after an abused kid gets some help, he doesn't feel like swearing as much, or he learns some alternative ways to express his anger. It would have been impossible to give an accurate description of residential life without the swearing. I hope some of the words, and they are only words, don't offend you.

Interestingly, this book chronicles two years of my life in residential treatment. In looking back over what I've written, I see a lot more swears in the intitial chapters. Hey, maybe I'm getting healthier. In chapter four, I get into a pretty weird discussion about feelings and swearing...it'll further clarify this issue.

Although I am admittedly a wee bit biased, I think this book will benefit people who work with children and families in residential treatment, yet may also be helpful reading for an even larger audience. Time will tell.

A lot of this book deals with residential treatment. For those new to the subject, abused and/or neglected dudes like me often react to their maltreatment by acting out. Big surprise. How would you act if you were repeatedly beaten and occasionally got it up the butt?

If the acting-out (i.e., bad behavior) in response to abuse and/or neglect becomes off-the-wall, we are often removed from our homes and placed in foster care, group homes, and/or residential treatment centers. When the big hand of the state first grabs us, attempts are generally made to place us in the "least restrictive environment." I was dropped off at a number of foster homes before my wicked ways finally forced my social worker to throw in the towel and place me in residential treatment.

I'm told foster and group homes, as well as residential treatment centers, are all ideally designed to help a kid and his/her family stabilize, work on issues, and then re-unite. Sometimes it ain't that simple. It wasn't for me, Jack.

Residential treatment centers, and there are lots

of them out there, take in the most troubled kids, the ones who act-out Big Time (e.g., hit, kick, bite, steal, tantrum, and piss on the enemy)! They are hard places to work and even harder to live in. Believe me, I know.

Looking inside the walls of residential treatment, as I do in this book, reveals some very extreme stuff, some incredibly powerful emotions and happenings. So get ready...you're in for a ride!

Oh yeah, almost forgot, the chapters of this book don't necessarily flow together. As stated, this didn't start out to be a book. But there is a progression. And many of the bases, I think, have been covered.

Friends, physical and sexual abuse is terrible. Neglect is often worse.

There are too many damn kids and adults walking around who have sufferred from these things. Enough is enough. This country has to stand up and say: "Cut the Shit!" That's what I think.

This book is my attempt to make a difference. Although I'm a sharp kid, I don't profess to have all the answers. At the very least, I hope this book gets you thinkin' about this stuff.

I gotta run, now. Promised my girlfriend I'd give her a call. Finally got a girlfriend. You see, anything's possible. Remember that.

1. What Do I Think About Residential Treatment: A Child's Perspective

This is an essay written by a fictitious character named Gus Studelmeyer. Gus, 13, has lived in a residential treatment center for three years. Inordinately freckled and a wee bit pudgy, Gus possesses an engaging smile—when there is occasion to smile. Lately, he has taken to spiking his red hair (orange—if you listen to Gus).

He never knew his father. His mother and her boyfriend (at the time) sexually and physically abused Gus over a period of three years, starting when Gus was two. When the courts got involved, Gus was placed with his maternal grandparents. He lived with them for two years before excessive tantrumming resulted in his first foster placement. After "disconnecting" with three successive foster families, Gus was placed at the Highland Hills Treatment Center for Boys, a residential child care facility for troubled youth.

I asked Gus if he would write an essay entitled: "What Do I Think About Residential Treatment." Oh yes, I forgot to mention...Gus has an IQ of 163...Gus is a genius.

What Do I Think About Residential Treatment

by

Gus E. Studelmeyer

Can you believe the E. stands for Elvis? Before you go throwing darts at my mom for what she and the asshole did to me, let me explain something. My mom had it pretty tough growing up. She was sexually abused by an uncle who lived in the house, off and on, for seven years. He threatened to kill her if she told. So she didn't until it was too late. In adolescence, drugs and alcohol were not unfamiliar to her. I was a mistake, born three days after her nineteenth birthday. I don't really like talking about this. Suffice to say, my mom has never been a happy camper. I'm still furious with her for abusing me and watching as that asshole hurt me. But I still love her. She will always be my mom. After not hearing from or seeing her for over five years, she suddenly appears one day at the Center. You figure it out. Mom actually got her act back together and wanted visiting to commence. That really pissed off a lot of the staff at Highland Hills because I was all set to try foster care again. Obviously, I viewed the situation with the utmost of ambivalence. Terribly conflicted, I took full advantage of the therapeutic milieu, to sort through and come to grips with this sudden curve life had so precipitously thrown. I now see my mom every other weekend, on Saturdays from noon to seven. The visits are no longer supervised—and hell, if we aren't talking about an overnight next month. Hey, I'm still pretty confused. I still think each visit might be the last one. And I have yet to really express my anger towards her. But Rome wasn't built in a day! O.K., enough about me. Let me tell you about residential treatment.

Your first day is a bitch. You're scared shit. Most kids can vividly recall the details of their first day—the staff who were on duty; the first kids they met; the social worker who brought them; how their room looked; I even remember the first thing I ate, a two-day old slice of apple pie. Man, did it taste good.

I wet the bed my first night. I didn't tell anyone. Some foster parents don't take kindly to boys who leak. At breakfast, my fragrance blew the deception. Margaret, the senior counselor, took me aside and told me that wetting the bed was no big deal. I tried to act cool, but boy was I relieved. (Hey, is that a play on words—or what?)

If I were running one of these places, I'd make sure a kid's first day was a good one. And that all the bases were covered.

After a while, a few things become very clear about residential treatment. First, it's safe. The staff don't hit the kids and there are heavy consequences for any kind of violence. This is good. Of course, in the beginning, it is the mission of every child to test this out. After all, most of us are unfamiliar with the concept of safety. I tantrummed pretty good. I remember one time kicking a staff member named Frank right in the balls. When he didn't strike back, I knew this was my kind of place.

Some kids "honeymoon" before "testing" commences. Not me. I went for the gusto.

Within a month or two, something else becomes clear about residential treatment: **POWER**. It permeates the environment. Kids are told what to do, when to do it, and why it should be done. Sure, there's autonomy built in, but the sense of powerlessness can become great. The temptation to misuse power, on the part of the staff members, hovers like a fly over shit. Sometimes I think the staff don't understand how powerful they are—and how that makes us feel.

Three times I've returned from school to find out my roommate had been changed. "The new combinations make more sense for the group," I get told. Screw You!! I hated Billy Parody. Rodney Jones farted all the time. And Carl Spooner was a certified looney. I ask you, the reader, how would you like to drive home one night and find out someone had moved your things across the street, and you were now living with Ed Magillicutty? You hate Ed Magillicutty! These kinds of things happen all the time in residential treatment. Most kids have already been subjected to the misuse of power prior to entering a treatment milieu. A lot of anger builds up due to this. Unless staff members are extremely sensitive to this issue, they risk maintaining a sense of alienation between the kids and themselves.

"Why?"
"Because I told you so!"

This kind of power makes me sick. I've always liked the staff members who didn't yell and gave reasons for things. "Because I told you so!" Who the hell do they think they are? And if we respond angrily to this

10

kind of power move we get in more trouble. **POWER-LESSNESS**. It sucks.

On a positive note, it doesn't take long after arriving before you find a new mother. It can be the cook, a counselor, your therapist, or even an older kid. You look for and find someone who seems special and maybe, just maybe, makes you feel special. Freud called this transference. (I read one of his books in the public library—I had to check out "penis envy"... thought I had it.)

It seems like all the kids here need to fill the void created by being separated from their moms. What's tough is that people don't stay too long in places like this. Just when you grow attached to and feel you can trust someone—they leave! It makes it tougher the next time around. I really liked Margaret O'Reilly. No, I loved Margaret O'Reilly. When she left it felt like I was being separated from my mom again. Margaret sent me a card on my birthday; it's still hanging over my bed.

If you work with kids who live away from their homes, you might become pretty important to some of them. I know it's a tough job (just ask Frank whom I kicked in the balls), but the longer you hang in, the better we do.

Occasionally, I've seen a staff member get overly attached to a kid. This starts out feeling pretty good to both of them, but usually causes a lot of problems. Most of us don't have what you consider "glowing" self esteem. If we see a staff member favoring a particular kid, it really pisses us off. "What am I, chopped liver?" becomes the popular sentiment.

Look, I know some of us can be quite difficult. I

11

was a hellion my first six months, considered quite obnoxious. But it was simply defensive posturing. (Can you say defense mechanism?) Kids aren't bad. They're just screwed up. The kid who's pushing you away the most is probably the one who needs you the most.

I think every residential facility would be better off if they never used such words as manipulative, lazy, uninvested, controlling, and obnoxious. They're pejorative adjectives. When you label one of us in such a way, you contaminate the waters and no one wants to swim with us anymore.

"Manipulative kids aren't fun to work with."
"They're a pain in the ass."
"Boy, is that kid MANIPULATIVE!!!"

Every time we get blasted for being "manipulative" (or any other such term), our self-concept suffers. We take on that word—we internalize a sense of badness. Yet the kid you call "manipulative" might have come to your facility with a history of "manipulating" his way out of getting beaten. So, maybe manipulating ain't so bad. Maybe, it simply needs to be understood in the context of a child's situation. Maybe people don't need to use these words anymore.

O.K., enough mumbo jumbo, let's talk SEX! (You Puritans in the audience can pass on the next few paragraphs.)

When you've been sexually abused, it's like your hormone switch gets turned on early. The abuse becomes an unwanted introduction to physical intimacy. In reality, the introduction is more like an invasion—

an invasion where the enemy never leaves. The scars of sexual abuse remain forever (at least, that's what my therapist says).

I've really had a hard time with this sex thing. And to be honest, so have the staff (well, not all of them— I exaggerate). But sometimes, it does appear that a bomb blast would be more acceptable to them than a blow job in the bathroom. Homosexual experimentation is a real no-no. C'mon, it's not like all of us are championing gay rights. Sexual experimentation is somewhat expectable.

Being a victim of sexual abuse means something BAD happened to you that was not in your control, "control" being the operative word here. I guess with some of us who have been dicked, the urge to replicate the sexual aggression, but this time from a "control" position, is rather great. It's a power thing. It's *mastery*. (I copped a look at some developmental literature, as well.) *Do "actively" to someone else what was accepted "passively" by you.*

We're told sexual feelings are normal, yet God help us if we act on them. Not to say this is an easy issue. It's not like I'm suggesting group orgies be allowed (well, maybe now and then). More sensitivity to biological expression would suffice.

Let's face it, some of us guys are at the perpetual hard-on stage. Some of us lose our minds during this period. Living at a treatment center for BOYS and not being adequately exposed (and I use the word lightly) to girls—is tough! I know the supervisors fear we'll impregnate the local girl scout troop if unleashed, but you can't hold back nature.

In reviewing what I've written thus far, it appears I

might be painting too negative a picture of residential care. Let's face it, most of us are angry dudes. When asked to talk about something, our anger often surfaces. We're particularly anti-authority (can you blame us?).

It's real hard to admit we like something or someone. We risk disappointment and/or rejection by committing our affection somewhere.

Most of us simply can't tolerate any more rejection. So you see a lot of face-saving and denial to avoid potential pain. A good staff member should be able to see through our "defenses" (I love that Sigmund guy).

I think most kids like the safety and security of residential care more than they let on. I'm big on moanin' and groanin':

"This place sucks, ya treat us like inmates."
"On my last day I'm gonna burn this place down."
(A particular favorite among the lads.)
"How would you like to live here?"
"Why don't you staff get a life?"

When you think about it, who else can we get mad at? Really. Scream at your mother and there's no visit next week. Swear at your teacher and you get suspended. Tell off your boss and you're history.

We can vent our anger within residential walls and still see daylight. It's wonderful (but don't expect us to admit it). Sometimes, a kid will leave the program less angry than when he came in. I think having the opportunity to continually blow off steam helps. It's a necessary evil. Although they often make me nauseous, angry outbursts usually result in "talks" about what is bothering us. I guess some of these "talks" prove beneficial (but don't tell the guys I've admitted this).

Continuing on a positive note, the sports and activities are great in residential treatment. I did more things in my first six months at Highland Hills than I had done in my entire life. No kiddin'.

Some of the sports I had never played before. Most kids are somewhat reluctant to try a sport they're not good at. Why risk the embarrassment and pain? At Highland Hills we had a super Activities Director, Neil. When it came time to play softball, Neil said there would be no striking out (God bless this man!). He said, "No striking out—it's spring training." In August, it was *still* spring training (you had to love this guy). Self confidence ain't big among the troops. People like Neil, who understand this, motivate us to try.

Three years ago, I couldn't hit a softball to save my life. Now, I plaster the damn ball. When I see that little white circle sailing over the left fielder's head I feel great! I don't feel like a loser. For kids like me, these are special moments. If it hadn't been for Neil, I'd still be on the sidelines. It's nice being part of the game.

I think every kid in residential care has lousy self-esteem. Most of us blame ourselves for the abuse and neglect we incurred. You have to love your parents. If they don't treat you right, *you* must be the problem.

Residential treatment tries to set the record straight. It attempts to stop us from blaming ourselves for any bad that occurred. The process involves bolstering our self-esteem and helping us come to terms with the reality of our individual situations.

You know, after I hit a home run—I feel great. I might even feel good the next day. If I have therapy on that day, I might even open up more—take a chance. It's funny how the two are connected. I just know it's hard to say certain things when I'm feeling shitty.

Speaking of therapy, what a cushy job. Some kids say they want to grow up and become child care workers. Not me. I want to be a therapist. Can you imagine getting paid to play and talk with kids? Child care workers have to deal with a lot of crap (remember Frank?). Therapists dress better; probably get paid more; and have the weekends off.

I've read some developmental literature. What a child care worker does is parent two-year-old behavior. I'm clear about this. Acting-out, obstinacy, tantrumming—all normal two-year-old behaviors— appear every day in a residential center. When kids improve and display three-, four-, and five-year-old behavior, they're discharged and a new two comes in. Like clockwork.

Who can parent two-year-old behavior year after year? Is it really such a mystery why child care workers don't last too long? It's a brutal job. No thank you, this guy is gonna be a therapist!

Look, I know I exaggerate. Some kids and parents would be pretty tough to meet with on a regular basis. Actually, I vaguely recall annihilating my first therapist's office. But he was a jerk and deserved the trashing. He forced me to talk about things I DIDN'T WANT TO TALK ABOUT! Shit, I still get mad when I think about him.

My second therapist, Ellen, has her act together. We play a lot of pool and card games. She isn't too aggressive on the talk front. But hell, if we don't do some great work together. I'm still not sure how she extracts it out of me. Even though I like her, there are times I don't want to meet. She's pretty cool about this.

At times, I get pissed off because she's pretty tight with the residential staff. If she has a safety concern regarding something I've said—right to the child care staff she goes. I guess on some level I appreciate this, but in general, it pisses me off.

Some of the other therapists in the building are know-it-alls. They clearly look down on the child care workers. Big mistake. If a kid can get a good rift going between his therapist and the child care staff, it's worth a lot of points (i.e., extra attention). There's nothing we enjoy more than good, old fashioned "splitting." It's no fun when *we're* the only ones upset.

Most kids in residential care are experts in the art of provocation. Plainly speaking, GETTING PEOPLE PISSED OFF! Staff members are sometimes hard to crack, but fellow inmates (kids) are EASY. Contrary to public opinion, there is real purpose behind peer antagonism.

You have to understand we're terrified of being "crazy." We've been poked and prodded by shrinks; analyzed, evaluated, assessed, tested, shmested... Catch my drift, reader? Ending up in a residential treatment center for EMOTIONALLY DISTURBED YOUTH does little to assuage our fears of insanity. So, how does one (like me) test the waters to prove he hasn't gone off the deep end? Well, it's not that difficult.

For example, Bruce, over there, goes wild when you call his mother a dyke. Say it and I guarantee he'll be tantrumming in five minutes. The kid is out to lunch. And when Brucie's going wild, all the other kids sit back and feel good. Why? Because, we're not as bonkers as Bruce. He becomes the yardstick. We can get upset, but as long as we don't act worse than Bruce, we're not crazy. *Bruce is crazy.* At times, we're all pretty good to him. We need Bruce.

Sometimes I wonder what ordinary kids dream about. What did Wally and the Beaver imagine each night? Me, I dream about being an ordinary kid.

"Ward, will you tell the boys to come down for dinner?"

"I'll be happy to, dear."

(Ward walks to the bottom of the stairs and looks up.)

"Boys, time for dinner. Wally, Beaver, GUS, c'mon down before it gets cold."

Wally, Beaver, and GUS. Boy, does that sound goooood! I'm pretty jealous of "ordinary kids" (like the Beave). I don't think they understand how wonderful they have it. Sometimes ordinary kids make fun of us residential dwellers. That really sucks. Let's trade places for one day!

Now and then I get nervous about telling an ordinary kid where I live. You never know how they'll react. I hate being embarrassed. I once decked a kid for making fun of Highland Hills. (Actually, he beat the crap out of me, I was taking poetic license.)

I've got to stop now, we're going roller skating in a few minutes. That means BABES! BABES!!!!!!!

Look, if you happen to come across a pudgy, red headed adolescent with a few zits, who lives in a residential treatment center but still looks like Tom Cruise, give him a break. He deserves it. He's trying. No shit.

2. The Restraint

For this chapter I've been asked to wear a wire. Yea, like in the cop movies. The author wants to intersperse my personal reflections with actual dialogue that typically occurs in a residential center. Sounds like an interesting concept.

It's been a number of months since I finished writing the first chapter. During this past year my mother got her act back together and visiting commenced for the first time in five years. After eight months of seeing her, a decision was finally made for me to return home. In fact, I'm going on a home visit in twenty minutes. My mother cancelled our last visit because of car problems.

Tape recorder on.

"My Mother cancelled our last visit because of car problems."

I'm reading out loud something I just wrote. It's now 10:10 a.m. She's 10 minutes late. Usually, she calls when she's going to be late. I hate when she's late. There's a car pulling in now. It could be her. Damn, it's Wayne, the maintenance man. It's now 10:20 a.m. She's really late.

"Where the heck is she?"

Maybe she's not coming. That would be two missed visits in a row. What the hell is going on here? The bitch is losing it again—I just know it. Where the hell is she?

"Maybe it's me?"

I always drove her crazy. Hell, I probably made her

drink. 10:22 a.m. 10:23 a.m. 10:25 a.m.

If she comes in the next 10 minutes, I won't get mad at her. I can't get mad at her. I don't want to blow it. Please, God, don't let me blow it.

"Gus."

"Yea."

"Before you go, could you please straighten up your room? It's a mess. I asked you nicely to take care of it an hour ago."

"Chris, my mother's coming in a second. I'll clean it when I get back."

"Gus, you know the rules, rooms need to be cleaned before visits. C'mon I'll give you a hand."

"I'm not doing it now. I told you, Chris, I'll clean it when I get back."

"Look, I know you're a little nervous about your mom being late, but the room has to be done now."

"Fuck you, asshole. I'm gonna stand here and wait for my mother. If you get near me, I'll knock the shit out of you."

"Gus, could you please go sit on your bed for awhile?"

"Make me, and this is what I'll do to you!"

"John, could you come over here? Gus just put his hand through the dry wall. We need to bring him to the Quiet Room."

"Get the fuck away from me. Don't touch me!"

"Can you walk with us?"

"Fuck you! Get away from me!.....ah....shit...fuck you...let go of my arms!! You're killing me....LET GO! LET ME GOOOO!!"

"O.K., let's put him on the floor."

"GET OFF ME...GET OFF OF ME!!!!"

"Take it easy, Gus."

"Get off me, assholes...what are you trying to do, hump me? FUCKIN' HOMOS!!! ....get off of me...you're breaking my arms...Jesus, don't hold me so hard...I can't breathe........I can't breathe!"

"You're O.K., Gus...take it easy."

"Get off..you're hurting me........GET OFF ME..............GET OFFFFFFFFF ME! I'LL KILL BOTH OF YOU WHEN I GET UP.....................GET OFFFFFFFF.....HELP! HELP!!!"

"John, hold his head, he's starting to bang it."

"LET GO OF MY HEAD!!!....I WON'T BANG IT...LET GO..OW..OW..LET GO! MA! MA! THEY'RE KILLING ME!.................................PLEASE.....LET GO....I CAN'T BREATHE!"

"Are you going to bang it anymore?"

"No, no, let go."

"O.K., John, take your hands off his head."

"Assholes.................I....hate it here..........I'll sue all you bastards............I..hate it here.........let me go................... let me go............................... CHILD ABUSE!....CHILD ABUSE!......................THEY'RE HURTING ME!....HELP!........ANYBODY!........child abuse.........they're hurting me........... hurting.... me.............get off...................."

"Take it easy, Gus."

"Get off.."

"That's it................just relax...............take a breath.............................don't worry, it's O.K. to cry...........we ain't macho, here.......................O.K., I'm going to let your arms go....................... good.............................all right, I'm getting off you now........why don't you lie here a few more

23

minutes.........................that's it."
"...............................She didn't come, did she?"
"No, she hasn't, and that stinks."
"Can I go sit on my bed?"
"Sure."

Tape recorder off.

Maybe this tape recording deal ain't such a great thing? Pretty intense, eh? Jesus, I haven't been physically restrained in over a year. I know it's a necessary evil, but boy does it suck. You lie helplessly on your stomach with your hands held perpendicular behind your back. The adult on top of you straddles his legs over yours. The more you struggle, the harder the "restrainer" pushes down. When this occurs, it sometimes gets hard to breathe (or, at least it feels that way).

You scream, you swear, you desperately try to scratch the restrainer's hands. Sometimes you lose it. You forget where you are. You forget who's holding you.

Sometimes the person holding you becomes the guy who raped and/or abused you—the swears, the taunts, the striking out. I think some of that is intended to provoke the restrainer into actually hurting us. Some of it is, of course, pure, unadulterated RAGE.

If we can get a child care worker to hurt us, the incident helps to solidify our poor self-image. New abuse reinforces the feelings that developed in response to the old abuse.

I think every kid in residential care has lousy self esteem, because on some level, he or she needs to believe the abuse that was incurred was deserved. We were abused because we were (and are) bad. We grow to believe this. After all, a kid can't figure out that abuse at the hands of a parent is the parent's mistake. Kids have to love their parents...stick up for them...be loyal...who else is there for us? If we were beaten, we deserved it. We were bad. We are bad. It's simple, Jack.

As I mentioned in the first chapter, residential treatment tries to set the record straight. We learn that any kind of abuse is wrong, but that the people who did it are not necessarily bad—they just did bad things...and need help. It's a hard pill to swallow. Some of us never quite digest it.

I hate to admit it, but I think some of us get restrained because we want to get held. We're perhaps feeling out of control, unloved, unwanted, lonely. Being held firmly can be quite comforting. There probably would be less restraints in residential care if there were more hugs.

Every kid needs attention. Abused kids need even more, but don't always know how to ask for it. A lot of us don't think we deserve it or anybody would want to give it. Hopefully, a kid will learn to "appropriately" seek attention in residential care and learn to feel good about himself. But when all else fails, a hand through the wall will get two hands around the body.

Some staff members are pretty quick to restrain a kid. I think it has something to do with "control." The BIG "C." We all want to be in control.

When we lose control we grow anxiety. I ain't big on anxiety. Most kids in residential care had bad things happen to them because they lacked control. They were helpless in the face of their abuse.

Staff feel the same way about control—each wants it and each seems to have a different threshold in terms of losing it.

Look, I know it's not always an easy decision—when to physically intervene with a kid—but it's a pretty damn serious intervention. People at times get hurt during restraints—both kids and staff. If I ran one of these places, I'd train my staff very carefully in this regard.

Now, of course, there are ways of getting back at those staff members who seem to delight in prematurely grabbing us. We once had a child care worker named Rudy. Rudy was an asshole with a short fuse. He'd put you on the floor if you just looked at him the wrong way. He'd hold you hard...and he'd hurt you. Not enough to get him reported, just enough to make your eyes water and your mouth spit. Before the agency canned the bastard—and there was a rumor about him being put on probation—we exacted our revenge.

Remember Brucie? In the first chapter, I talked about our fear of being "crazy." I wrote about this kid, Bruce, who tantrummed at our slightest provocation. I commented on how good we all felt—how "normal" we all felt—when Brucie went wild. Kids in residential care need mates like Bruce. One "wacko" dude makes us all look and feel better.

Calling Bruce's mother a dyke used to set him off, but now we've got a new one. Last summer, Bruce was caught playing with himself in a movie theater. So lately, whenever we want to get a rise out of him (excuse the expression), we call him "Pee Wee." He goes bonkers.

When Rudy was starting to really piss us off, one of us got the idea to employ Bruce. (For you squeamish ones in the audience, you might want to skip the next few paragraphs—they're slightly indelicate.)

The goal was clear: Get Rudy out. The plan was ingenious. Conceived after tuck-in one hot, steamy night, with the aid of contraband devil dogs and Dr. Pepper (yeah, I'm a pepper, you're a pepper), it involved Bruce and it was messy. We loved it. To make a long story short, we each paid Bruce a buck if he would get restrained by Rudy every time he, Bruce, had to take a crap! The plan was beautiful in its simplicity. Although the house stunk for two weeks Rudy soon vanished. We hated Rudy. We loved Brucie. We needed Brucie. Although I guess it's not very nice that we took advantage of him.

Most kids in residential care, at least in their first year of treatment, really need to look out for number one—no one else ever has. If exploiting another kid fills a need, like in this case the need not to be judged "crazy," then we go after the sucker. Maybe, in the second year, we'll talk about better ethics.

Anyways, our plan to terminate Rudy worked. I guess we have more control than we think.

Tape recorder on.

"Gus, you doing O.K.?"

"Yeah, Chris, I'm all right."

"Can we talk?"

"Who are you, Joan Rivers?"

"Glad you haven't lost your sense of humor."

"Never."

"Hey, that was a tough scene. You were pretty upset."

"My damn mother. Two visits in a row she's missed—without a call."

"That's pretty lousy. You feel like something's going on?"

"I'm feeling like it's falling apart. She's slipping back."

"What were the last few visits like? You didn't talk much about them."

"Not so great. She seemed more on edge, more nervous. I think she's having trouble at work, and I found some Southern Comfort under the sofa."

"Doesn't sound too good."

"It sucks. I'm scared and I'm pissed."

"You're scared and you're pissed—who can blame you? It's too bad we couldn't have talked like this before the fireworks."

"It was building up inside of me. I just couldn't handle what was going on. Guess I'll be working to pay off that hole in the wall?"

"Yup, you're in debt, man. Gus, you were really upset. We had to hold you pretty good. Are you O.K. about what went on?"

"Sure, I understand how things work."

"You know, we don't like having to hold kids like that. It's not fun for anyone."

"It was for Rudy."

"Until you paid Bruce."

"You knew about that?"

"Rudy was in the wrong business, and Bruce would have done it for nothing. You guys should lay off Bruce."

"Damn, you guys know everything!"

"Not everything. We still haven't figured out who snuck in the devil dogs."

"Seriously, Chris, I know you care, and I appreciate the way you talk with me. You're a good guy."

"Thanks, Gus. We're tryin'."

Tape recorder off.

Up close and personal, aye. When I was approached about wearing a wire, I never thought you'd be hearing voices from the floor. But, what the hell, that's residential treatment. It ain't always pretty.

Physical restraint happens—it probably happens more than it should. It's a damn serious intervention.

When I first came to the Hills, I was a terror. I often lost control and needed to be held. But other kids have come to the center with less anger and more control. Such kids don't need physical interventions. But some of them get it, anyway—because they learn the routine. They follow the crowd. They jump on the bandwagon:

29

Friends, if you're feeling lonely, angry, or just plain shitty don't hold it in. Don't wait to talk to someone. No, friends, the answer is: GET RESTRAINED. Yes, for only a temporary consequence, you, too, can be thrust on the floor and held like a bloomin' idiot. You'll get attention, notoriety, and the physical intimacy you so desperately crave. It's like a drug! It feels good! Buy it! C'mon down!!!!

It really shouldn't be this way. Troubled kids should be put with normal kids so they don't learn more bad habits—like getting restrained when you don't need to be.

Look, if you happen to work with kids in residential treatment, be careful. We only come through once. We weren't born bad. If you have to touch us, remember, a hug feels pretty good, yet, the floor is often cold. You owe it to us to know what you are doing.

You've got a really hard job—I'd never do it. I used to think about becoming a therapist—but that ain't easy, either. Executive Director, Gus E. Studelmeyer, now that sounds pretty good.......

"Director Studelmeyer?"

"Yes?"

"Some of the boys were caught eating devil dogs after tuck-in last night."

"What do you think we should do?"

"What we should have done a long time ago."

"And what's that?"

"Fire Rudy.....and break out the Pepper!!"

3. Foster Care

Life goes on for old Gus. After my Mom cancelled a slew of home visits and a number of appointments with my therapist, the writing on the wall gradually turned to graffiti. I saw it coming. I'm not sure I wanted it to work. Too much history. It's not like I had a choice. She was, and is, my mother. I gave it my best shot, and maybe she did, too. Now it's foster care, again—or prepare for independent living. Life sucks.

I guess my Mom just wasn't cut out for the June Cleaver thing. I have to accept that (I'm told). Yet I have so many mixed feelings. At times, rage dominates. ("I can't believe I punched my hand through the wall"), while on other occasions loneliness and despair flood the old cerebrum.

Maybe when I'm 18 and have my act together, we'll "re-unite." I've seen a lot of kids leave this place over the years. Sooner or later, they all seem to end up back home, no matter how bad it was—or is. Blood is thicker than crap, I guess.

Intellectually, I can grasp the concept that I must rise above the rubble of my past (not Barney), but to do so I will need fuel...sustenance...reason! And where does one like me find such energy? Why should I or any kid in my situation—and there are lots of us dudes—be hopeful? Remember, I've already blown out of three foster homes, and before that, I was abused at home.

Being hopeful implies we expect something good to happen. When you've been bounced around and abused, you don't expect good to happen, because good only happens to "good" people. The "other" people. Not us. Not me.

My life has been one long series of disconnections. Like a car getting gas, if the nozzle never stays in long enough (keeps getting jerked) you (it) don't go very far. Unless, of course you come upon a new station in life that supplies the fuel without interruption (quite rare in these here parts).

The road is hard, damn hard. Each new station begins to look like the first, the one that caused your original engine trouble. The tendency is to pull out before someone starts jerkin' the nozzle again. It's a lousy pattern. You keep leavin' with that empty feeling, but at least you pay a little less. I think "emptiness" is quite pervasive among the troops.

Such is the life of a damaged child. We are all empty and require lots of filling...but when the filling starts we often panic and attempt to sabotage the fuel intake. The pain of having it precipitously shut off, AGAIN, is the worst kind of pain. Better to sabotage and end things yourself than have the fuel stop without warning.

So, is there no hope for me and my comrades? Does the path leading from abuse and neglect only go in one direction—South? Hell No! But to rise above the muck takes hard work and luck!

Those of us who end up in foster care and/or residential treatment need to have the right kind of people battling for and with us. People who constantly try to fill our tanks, even in the face of treacherous fireworks.

Such people need to truly understand who we are and "where we are coming from" (I love that term—what did they write in the 60's?). Such information enables helpers to form reasonable expectations concerning our behavior and personalities. It enables them to stick by us when the going gets rough.

I've seen a lot of kids blow out of foster care because the foster parents over-reacted to the kid's behavior. They had no clue what that kid was about—and no one was filling them in. I think, however, foster parents get a bad rap. The problem is in the training and support, or lack thereof. But then again, you can't go blaming the state social service departments, the people in charge of overseeing foster parents, because they'll just cry poverty. I know this, I read the papers. I face it first hand when my yearly clothing allowance gets cut.

Then who do you blame? I don't know. Maybe Reagan, Bush, and the "me" generation of the 70's. Maybe there just aren't enough people in this country who give a damn about their fellow man.

Wow, I really got off on a tangent, eh? Man, I'm all screwed up and wired. Just thinking about foster care again evokes massive Kah-Kah! I can't believe I'll be going through it, again.

Man, I'm really getting tired. It's a few minutes before bedtime and I need some z's. I'll try...I'll try and...(yawn)...write a few more limes, no lines... gotta...gotta put some jokes in...(yawn)...seems too...serious...(what's going to happen to me?)...I'm sleepy...sleepy...

"Gus."

"Yes, Director Pittsiotti."

"I'd like you to meet your new foster parents, Jill and Orville Bradey."

Gus: The Bradeys, no shit! What was wrong
        with the Cleavers?
Jill: We're so happy to finally meet you, Gus.
        Here, would you like some chocolate chip
        cookies? I baked them myself.
Gus: Are they real chocolate chips or carobs?
Jill: Chocolate chips.
Gus: Good. The cook here turned holistic last
        year. I'm sick of her "natural" crapola.
        Mmmmm...these are great!
Orv: Gus, we've got a room all set up for
        you. T.V., video player, CD, phone,
        Apple computer, and nintendo. We
        hope you'll like joining our family.
Gus: I'm warming up to the idea.
Dir. Pittsiotti:
        Gus, the Bradeys have no other children
        and recently won the grand prize in the
        State's lottery.
Gus: Getting hot, very hot.
Jill: Gus, do you have any questions for us?
Gus: Yea, one, the big one. Are you two gonna
        dump me like all the other foster parents
        did?
Orv: Gus, we'll never give up on you. Never.
Gus: But what if I act up—Big Time? Steal your
        car, french kiss your grandmother, eat jello
        with my hands?
Jill: (smiling) We expect you to test us. To see if
        we'll be like all the others.
Orv: We know if it starts feeling good in our
        household, you'll probably panic—
Jill: —try to sabotage the placement before we

34

	end it. Isn't that the typical pattern?
Orv:	I guess it all comes down to expectations......
Jill:	...we know what to expect.
Orv:	We know there will be hard times.
Jill:	And we know that talk is cheap. Words mean little. Trust is earned.
Orv:	We'll need to practice what we preach....and we shall.
Jill:	Bet on it.
Gus:	Sounds good. But what if you die?
Orv:	We won't die, Gus.
Gus:	You won't die?
Orv:	Dir. Pittsiotti, tell him.

Dir. Pittsiotti:

> Gus, Jill and Orville are the best foster parents in the world. Just like in the old "Newlywed" game, they are a "gift" (family) chosen just for you. Nothing can go wrong. No disruptions, no deaths.

Gus: Wow, I'm freakin'! This is hard to believe. I've never had a break in my life. Someone's changed the script. This can't be happening.

Dir. Pittsiotti:

> It's real, Gus. They will be with you for as long as you need them.

Gus: I've been sexually abused. My whole orientation to intimacy has been skewed. Most foster parents freak when the sexual acting out commences—even the best ones. You ready for that?

Jill: Gus, my aunt is Dr. Ruth.

Orv:	—and in the 60's, I was an active nudist.
Jill:	(gazing confidently at Orville) We have travelled the many roads of human sexuality. We are both comfortable we can handle your driving.
Gus:	OOH, I like the way you put that. A little play on Freud. Nice touch.
Jill:	Thank you.
Gus:	And what about my mother?
Orv:	She's your mother, and she'll always be your mother.
Gus:	Hey, I've written that before.
Jill:	I know, we've enjoyed your articles.
Gus:	Really?
Orv:	Gus, we won't reject you, even if you kick me in the balls.
Gus:	Guess you read about poor Frank. I still feel bad about that.
Jill:	Your Mom will always be welcome in our household, and you can visit her as you see fit.
Orv:	We're not going to compete against your mother. That would be wrong. We're all on the same team. The "Gus" team.
Gus:	Yo Team!
Jill:	If it makes sense for the two of you to be re-united, we'll do everything we can to make that a reality.
Gus:	Can I go to college?
Jill:	We've secured a scholarship to Harvard for you. But where you go will, of course, be your choice.
Gus:	Fuckin' A!

Orv: We prefer you not swear. It gets kids in trouble.

Gus: So, you'll give me consequences when I act devilish?

Jill: Sure.

Orv: But, we'll explain why every consequence is given and, if possible, we'll let you be part of deciding the correct form of discipline.

Gus: What if I become physically aggressive towards one or both of you?

Jill: We, like Superman, are from the planet Krypton. We can't be hurt.

Gus: You are now yankin' my chain. You expect me to believe you both have—super powers? Please...

Orv: Gus, with my x-ray vision, I can see the contents of your pocket. In it you have 3 dollars and 43 cents;

Jill: —a Nolan Ryan baseball card;

Orv: —and one, slightly used cond—

Gus: Okay, Okay, what the hell. You've made your point. I believe. But what about Kryptonite?

Orv: We've developed an immunity to it.

Gus: Gosh. You guys are everything a kid could want in foster parents.

Dir. Pittsiotti:
         Gus, they're the best!

Gus: But what about my pain?

Jill: You mean inside?

Gus: Yea. Will you—can you—make it go away? X-ray it to the phantom zone?

Orv: Do you want it to go away? Do you want us to erase all of your bad memories?

Jill: Would you like a fresh start?

Gus: You can do that?

Orv & Jill:
    Gus, we're the best, remember?

Dir. Pittsiotti:
    Would you like a fresh start, Gus?
    Would you like the Bradeys to implant a different set of memories?

Gus: Hmmm. Let me think about that. Could I have another cookie while I'm thinkin'?

Jill: We made them just for you, Gus.

Dir. Pittsiotti:
    Well, do you want your slate cleaned?

Gus: ...No, I don't think so. As terrible as I've had it, that would be like giving up. Part of me thinks I can work through the muck. I'm not a quitter. But sometimes the pain gets real bad and I feel like such a loser. As if I brought it all on myself.

Orv: We know that, Gus. Most kids in your situation feel that way.

Jill: When the pain gets bad—we'll be with you.

Orv: We'll always be with you.

Gus: What if my acne never clears and I get fatter?

Jill: Our x-ray vision will cure your acne.

Orv: And if you get fatter—there will just be more of you to love.

Gus: You guys are unreal!

Dir. Pittsiotti:
    They're the best!

Gus: Can my friends at Highland Hills come and visit, as well as some of the child care workers?

Orv: Of course.

Gus: Can my roommate, Hector, do sleepovers?

Jill: Absolutely, if it's okay with Mr. Pittsiotti and Hector's mother.

Gus: Will I get an allowance?

Orv: $10.00 a week.

Jill: If you do your chores.

Gus: Can I smoke cigarettes?

Orv: Do you really want to smoke?

Gus: Damn right, I do.

Jill: Even if you'll die of lung cancer at the early age of 43—

Orv: —after 2 operations and 10 painful months of chemotherapy?

Gus: What...you can read the future?

Orv & Jill:
    Gus, we're the—

Gus: —best...I remember. O.K., to hell with the smoking. I mean, I will choose not to smoke.

Orv: Good decision.

Gus: When do you guys plan to take me? Will I have time to "terminate", as they say in the business?

Jill: We know how important it is to say good-bye.

Orv: You can't say hello...

Jill: ...until you say good-bye.

Gus: Hey, you've got that down pretty—

Jill: —good.

Orv: We practice a lot, remember—
Gus: I know...I know...you're the best.
Dir. Pittsiotti:
         Well, Gus, what do you think?
Gus: I think Lady Luck has finally flown my
         way. This sounds almost too good to
         believe. Let's go for it.
Orv & Jill:
         Great!
Gus: One last question.
Jill: Yes.
Gus: Will I have to clean my room?
Orv: Only if you want too. We have a maid who
         has been with us, the Bradeys, a long
         time.
Gus: Let me guess, her name's Alice, right?
Jill: Why, yes, how did you know?
Gus: Just lucky, I guess.

"Gus, Gus, wake up. You fell asleep at the desk...
Gus..."
"Just lucky I guess...just lucky I guess...jussss..."
"Wake up, Gus."
"Wha...what...Where am I?"
"Gus, I think you were dreaming."
"Hector, is that you?"
Hector: No, it's Bart Simpson. Who the hell do you
         think it is?
Gus: Hector, I'm getting out of here. The
         Bradeys and Alice are going to be my new
         foster family. They said you can do
         overnights!
Hector: Gus, wake-up, man, you were dreaming.

This is Highland Hills and you ain't goin'
nowhere.

Gus: It wasn't a dream! I'm going! And don't
use those double negatives anymore. What
are you going to do without me?

Hector: Gus, you're 14 1/2 years old. You live at
Highland Hills. Your mother just blew
you off. Now, you've got to hope for
something new—like a goddamn miracle.
Because most foster parents want young
and attractive. Pimples, fat, adolescent,
that's not what people are looking for. You
know that.

Gus: Shit! It was such a great dream. They were
the best.

Hector: The Bradeys. The Bradeys? After
Marsha, what was there?

Gus: They were really cool about me having
contact with my mother.

Hector: Sure, sure, and I suppose they were
gonna send you to Yale?

Gus: No, Harvard. And they would never reject
me. And, beat this, they would never die.

Hector: Gus, wake-up, this is the real world—it
ain't "Cocoon."

Gus: I loved that movie.

Hector: But that was fantasy...this is real.

Gus: God, it sucks waking up.

The preceeding dialogue between Hector and yours
truly, as well as the "dream sequence," were tran-
scribed from memory. Remember, I'm a genius.
Boy, you don't have to be Freud to figure out where

I'm coming from (there's that line, again). I'm scared shit about my future. I've read that in adolescence we're supposed to be "separating", forging a new identity. How the hell can I, or kids like me, get on with the process—get on with LIFE—when our past is so unresolved. You can't jump off a diving board if there's a crack in it. Well, I've got cracks, no, I've got crevices, everywhere. Wherever I go, if in fact I do go, gets me and the crevices. God, life is such a bitch.

Hey, that was one helluva dream. I would have enjoyed meeting Alice. She seemed like such a hot ticket. And having my pimples obliterated by x-ray vision, man, we're talkin' teenage heaven.

I've been through foster care before. It's a real crapshoot. Sure, there are some great foster parents out there; I've heard of a few, but as mentioned previously, most don't get the kind of training they truly require and, therefore, many lack the sophistication to care for "troubled" children. (I hate being labeled "emotionally disturbed"—who decides when we are not disturbed anymore?)

It appears to take at least a year (minimum) for someone to become a competent child care worker— to care for troubled kids. A year full of comprehensive training and hands-on experience. Foster parents, who are asked to "parent" troubled kids often coming from residential treatment centers, seem to get one-tenth the training a child care worker receives (if that), yet are asked to parent the child FULL TIME, at times with little support. It really doesn't make sense. It's not like we're "cured" when someone designates us "ready" for foster care. Life will always be tough. The emotional work never ends for an abused and/or neglected lad—bet on that.

My therapist would be proud of me for expressing my feelings so articulately. (Actually, she is proud of me—I copped a look at her progress notes—it didn't take a "genius" to sneak into her office...if it did I'd still get in.) But these words and a dime still won't get me a cup of coffee. I hate to sound so pessimistic.

There are indeed foster care success stories. In spite of my venting, I'm not giving up hope that I'll be one of them. I've got some good people at the Hills rooting for me. There are people here who believe in me—they're supplying the fuel. I'm getting filled. But every now and then, it feels like I'm playing the game of life against a stacked deck. Every day that goes by without a change, in my case, hurts.

It doesn't have to be this way. Maybe when I'm older I'll try to do something about the foster care problem. Find a way to pay and train them accordingly.

But right now, I'm more interested in getting laid and having a good time. Jesus, I'm going to be 15 in five months. I've got some experimenting to do. I've got to rise above the rubble and do some living. HEY, WILMAAA!!!

4. "Feelings"

I just finished reading Stephen King's *Four Past Midnight*. King is popular among the troops. It's mastery. We've had such horrific things done to us, it's kind of soothing and therapeutic to read about someone else getting chewed alive and/or gutted by a fireball. The King-man let's us control the terror. (Maybe for the first time.) We buy the books (if we choose). We read them (at our discretion). And we finish them unscathed (at times). It's beautiful. ("Someone else, besides me, is going crazy.")

I think most abused children have an inexorable fascination with the dark side, the supernatural, the unknown. Defensively, we tend to rely on these "unknown" forces for the cause of our misery. It would be too simple—and too damn painful—to blame our parents for the emotional havoc they inflicted or contributed to. And although most of us disturbos tend to blame ourselves for all the bull that has occurred, we're always looking for an "out". It's easier to look elsewhere for "cause" (and blame). That's when the dark side is revealed.

Many troubled children believe they have the devil lurking inside of them.

"I got beaten because of the devil inside of me."
"The devil makes me do bad things."
"I think the devil is inside my mother, too."

In reality, it's a nice way of getting people off the hook. All blame falls on the devil (and he could care less).

Well, getting back to King, *Four Past Midnight* is a collection of four pulsating stories that disrupt your emotional rhythm. It's not his best work (yo, "Stand"), but it helped me through a tough period.

The second story is called " Secret Window, Secret Garden." I don't want to give the plot away but, briefly, the story involves a popular fiction writer who is confronted by an unsettling stranger who accuses the writer of plagiarizing one of his stories. Is the stranger real or a figment of the writer's imagination? Legitimate dude or alter ego? King, of course, keeps us in suspense until the very end, as he weaves a chilling tale of baleful delight.

A damned good story, Stevo—and for me, quite evocative...

As you know, I'm a fictitious character. I have no rights, no privileges, no control. When the writer wants me to say or do something, I comply. (Give me your paw, Gus, that' a boy!)

If you have read the previous chapters, you were allowed a deep and penetrating look into my psyche. You read about my history, you were there when I tantrummed and got restrained, you experienced my tears, and in the last chapter I exposed my fear and ambivalence about foster care. I'm continually turned inside out.

Well, buckos, King's story got me thinking. Actually, it got me irritated!

Who is this guy who created me? What's his angle? Are the opinions that flow from my mouth mine or his? How come I get turned inside out every chapter and he walks away smelling like a rose (and then gets all the credit)? Is he hiding behind me? I'm getting pissed! Even a fictitious character wants his own identity. I want to know, know now, where the author ends and Gus (me) begins? I want some boundaries, man. I won't be used. I don't care if the author has me commit suicide in the next chapter or step in dog shit, it's time for a confrontation.

"Hey, you, with the moustache and brillo pad head, I want to talk to you."

"My name is Charlie — you know that."

"Yes, of course I know. In fact, your full name is Charles D. Appleberg."

"Don't get wise...it's Appelstein."

"Excuse me, I'm upset."

Charlie: You know, I shouldn't be talking to you like this.

Gus: Why?

Charlie: Because you're fictitious. You don't exist. I made you up.

Gus: Fuck-you. That's a cop-out.

Charlie: You don't have to swear. I get criticized about your language. Why don't you tone it down?

Gus: Fuck-you.

Charlie: Cut it out!

Gus: I'll cut it out if you promise to stick around and talk.

Charlie: O.K., but this is ridiculous. I'll be talking to myself.

Gus: Will you? That's exactly what I want to find out.

Charlie: What do you mean?

Gus: I mean...how much of me is you?

47

Charlie: I'm all you. You don't exist.

Gus: You're not catching my drift, Chuck.

Charlie: Don't call me Chuck—I hate that name.

Gus: Let me explain the situation. In the first chapter, for instance, you have me decree that I hate when people misuse power,
"Why?"
"Because I told you so.'"
Remember...

Charlie: Of course I remember, I wrote those lines.

Gus: Well then, do I (Gus), your noble representative of residential treatment, really hate the misuse of power? Or is the opinion overstated and maybe more representative of your own issues around authority and POWER?

Charlie: Stupid question. The Gus chronicles aren't about me, they're about you—and who you typify.

Gus: Bullshit! Are you stating that you or anyone else can truly write passionately about kids like me, their families, and their stay in residential care objectively? You can do this without your own feelings and history getting in the way? That's bull; you know better.

Charlie: What's your point?

Gus: My point, your Heinass, is obvious. It's fuckin' easy—

Charlie: Hey!

Gus: It's friggin' easy to do what you're doing.

Charlie: And what is that?

Gus: You create a character, me, and chapter after chapter, pull his strings without acknowledging or taking any responsibility for how your own issues and feelings might be influencing his words and actions.

Charlie: The readers don't want to know and certainly don't care about my personal issues and motivations...they're immaterial. Since when are fiction writers required to bare their souls? Does Stephen King tell you how it feels to write each story—and why?

Gus: Knock, knock, 'Hello in there.'

Charlie: Hey, don't touch me!

Gus: Touch you? I can't. I'm fictitious, remember? Feeling on edge Chuck?

Charlie: Please do not call me CHUCK!

Gus: Sorry, I tend to get provocative when I'm hungry. Do you think we could call a temporary truce and order some Domino's pizza?

Charlie: You can't be hungry—you have no stomach. I'm not calling Domino's.

Gus: O.K., fine, I'm not real—but I'm still hungry! So go to your keyboard and type me up a big juicy steak, smother it in gravy and give me a side of fried peppers and onions.

Charlie: O.K., no problem, one steak coming right up...

Gus was famished. He ordered a big juicy steak—the waiter brought it out. Gus feverishly severed the first succulent piece and triumphantly brought it to his mouth. Tears of joy began to roll down his face. He would chew it slowly, he would remember this moment "Shit, what the fuck!" Like a volcanic eruption, the contents of Gus' mouth violently discharged onto his unsuspecting lap. "It's liver! I hate fuckin' liver!"

Gus had been duped.

Charlie: HA HA HA—sometimes, I just amaze myself.

Gus: Was that your idea of a joke?

Charlie: I told you not to call me Chuck—keep it up and I'll have you snorting sushi.

Gus: O.K., O.K., let's get back to the issue at hand.

Charlie: Good idea.

Gus: Feelings, man, that's what I'm talking about. Nothing more than feelings.

Charlie: I used to love that song!

Gus: You dudes who work with kids or teach how to do it can't pretend you don't have feelings.

Charlie: I don't think people do that.

Gus: Give me a break! If a child care worker comes in after having a fight with his babe the kids suffer. And if we complain about his mood, he denies it and probably gets angrier.

Charlie: It could happen.

Gus: And if one of the child care workers had a hurtin' childhood, it sometimes will show. There's that risk.

Charlie: So, what are you trying to say?

Gus: It's brutal working with bonker boys like me. We push your buttons. We get under your skin. That's our mission. To see if you'll screw us over like the people who initially did. We're trying to make sense of the world. Can adults be trusted? Am I good or bad? etc., etc. We've got big questions that only you can answer.

Charlie: And if we don't have our act together, can't look inside, the answer might come out wrong.

Gus: Precisely.

Charlie: Therapists sometimes refer to this as "counter transference."

Gus: Jack, I don't care what they call it, I only care about people in child care recognizing it. It pisses me off when child care workers poke and prod my feelings while denying their own. I've seen some pretty good workers wilt under the heat because they couldn't show the old vulnerability.

Charlie: Are you pointing a finger at me?

Gus: Yea, the middle one.

Charlie: Why?

Gus: Because you haven't had the guts to examine how much of me is really you. Not all kids in residential treatment talk and act like me. Where are you taking poetic license and WHY? What's inside of you that makes me tick? C'mon, dude, model some vulnerability. If you want folks in this field to pay more attention

to, what did you call it? Counter transference? Then it's got to start with you!

Charlie: Sure you don't want another pizza?

Gus: I'm waiting.................

Charlie: How about if I get you laid in the next
chapter?

Gus: waiting.....................................still...
waiting.

Charlie: O.K., O.K., I'll talk—but it won't be easy.

Gus: This stuff ain't ever easy.

Charlie: Well, first of all, I really do believe you
are, in fact, quite representative of kids
in residential treatment.

Gus: ....waiting....still waiting..............now
startin' to feel like that damn little bunny
in the Eveready commercials.

Charlie: All right, I catch your drift. Not every
kid would write about residential treatment and use as many swears as you do.

Gus: Hmmm. That's interesting! So where are
my swears coming from?

Charlie: That's personal.

Gus: Whad'ya mean?

Charlie: I have a hunch where your (my) swears
come from. Probably has something to
do with displaced anger. But that's for me
to deal with. Giving you a proclivity
towards the four-letter word hasn't de-
tracted from getting your message across.
At work, I constantly have to be aware of
any demons I might harbor getting into
the work space. If I blow an interaction
due to some unresolved baggage or

inappropriate feelings, I have to take responsibility and apologize. And try to learn from the mistake. If I or anyone else blows too many interactions due to undetected baggage getting through, it's time for professional assistance. I'm serious about this. Psychotherapists and others engaged in emotional helping professions are often encouraged to be in therapy themselves. There shouldn't be a stigma associated with this. Working day to day with people who are hurting can, and often does, bring out the hurt in ourselves. To be truly effective, one has to be aware of this reality. I don't believe people can consistently and effectively assist others without truly being in touch with their own issues and history.

Gus: Man, can you sling it!

Charlie: Hey, up until this chapter you did all the talking.

Gus: That speech you just gave. Sounded a bit touchy-feely, Kemosabe.

Charlie: Then let me make this perfectly clear. I think it's essential for child care workers and therapists to know where they're coming from. To display strong "observing egos." In other words, they must possess the ability to take a step back and psychologically observe what they are doing. And if where they are "coming from" (sound familiar?) needs some repair, they should seek some fixing.

53

However, I always make it clear that it is not the role of the child care supervisor to do therapy with the child care staff. Child care workers are taught to be aware of the psychological traps inherent in the position, but are instructed to "check their baggage at the door" before every shift.

Child care supervisors and trainers should teach their workers to anticipate experiencing a myriad of feelings that this work elicits, feelings such as hate, anger, sexual attraction, frustration, etc. By matter-of-factly normalizing these common feelings, the child care worker will be significantly less distraught when some occur.

Gus: Nine long sentences without a joke! You're puttin' us to sleep, Jack.

Charlie: Sorry, got carried away.

Gus: So, Gus, yours truly, has a lot of you in me?

Charlie: Actually, there's quite a lot of me in him. I mean you.

Gus: But Who's on first?

Charlie: I don't know.

Gus: No, he's at second!

Charlie: No, No is at third!

Gus: So, besides being a teaching fool, I mean tool, I'm also kind of an alter ego, on whose shoulders you displace some of your baggage?

Charlie: Correct. And it's O.K. for me to do so as long as I don't distort what you have to say.

Gus: God, this means we're a lot alike.

Charlie: Shit, I never really thought about that.

Gus: Whoa! You swore, good buddy. What about the goody two shoes image?

Charlie: Forget the image. I'm not so sure I want to be identified with a chubby, zit-faced, emotionally disturbed adolescent!

Gus: But I have an I.Q. of 163!

Charlie: Still, this might not look so good.

Gus: Maybe the major parts of you in me aren't so much the disturbed aspects, but the personality traits?

Charlie: Hmmm. Interesting point. Could, in fact, be a life saver.

Gus: Even though I'm a screwed-up kid, we can still share similar personality traits (like being loud, funny and passionate) without me completely impugning your reputation.

Charlie: Hey, why did you use the term 'screwed-up' instead of fu-k-d up, like you normally would?

Gus: I don't know. Maybe we're resolving some things. Maybe I'm (we're) a little less angry.

Charlie: This is weird.

Gus: Ya know, they say it's pretty hard to change one's personality. Adolescents with personality disorders—(I was looking at the DSM III, checking out sexual

addiction. Missed it by one criteria!)
Adolescents with personality disorders
aren't gonna change too much. They say
you can only modify a personality.
*Maybe our similarities point out how
difficult it is to give up what's comfortable.* You gave me a personality somewhat similar to your own because it was
more comfortable to write me in your
image. Maybe this little discourse on
personality could be helpful to the reader.

Charlie: Interesting points. People tend to do what
they are "comfortable" doing, even when
what is "comfortable" might be less effective. A conservative therapist might not
want to do home visits. A behavioristic
child care worker might resist his/her
program abolishing its level system. A
Residential Director might be uncomfortable about parents spending significant
blocks of time on the units, etc., etc.

Gus: Kids might be—and are—uncomfortable about giving up behavior patterns
that have served their needs.

Charlie: And none of these people are bad.

Gus: It's human nature, Jack.

Charlie: Change is a bitch. But to be effective—

Gus: —We've got to embrace it.

Charlie: In the long run, it will be our friend.

Gus: And as for our personalities?

Charlie: I hope we've made it clear that they can
only change so much. And that it's real
important to understand that. Child care

workers have burned out over kids they expected to change. I've seen it happen.

Gus: Faulty expectations, eh?

Charlie: Yup. That's why training is so critical.

Gus: I don't buy it.

Charlie: Buy what?

Gus: Buy that you can't radically change one's personality—be it dysfunctional or not.

Charlie: Gus, it's a given. It's a done deal.

Gus: Okay, Charles, I won't argue with you.

Charlie: Charles?

Gus: Yes, Charles, pardon me for using nick names and profanities. I'm terribly mortified by my previous actions.

Charlie: Mortified?

Gus: Yes. I've decided to turn a new leaf. I'm giving up red meat, planting trees in the inner cities, and staying comfortable in my own space. Can you dig this, man?

Charlie: Yea, I see where you're going. I'm with ya, Gus. We won't be loud anymore.

Gus: Correct.

Charlie: We won't use sarcasm.

Gus: Never.

Charlie: And no more sexual innuendos.

Gus: Perish the thought.

Charlie: It's mellow time.

Gus: Right. We're now just two laid-back, easy-going brothers.

Charlie: Yes, this feels good. C'mon, let's chant or something.

Gus: And they said you can't change personality.

Charlie: You think they're buying this?

Gus: Fat chance.

Charlie: That's what I thought.

Gus: Good. Then let's get loud and eat something that's bad for us.

Charlie: Sounds great!

Gus and Charlie bought some greasy hamburgers and.......

Gus: WAIT A SECOND!! I've been down this road before. No more fuc-, I mean, no more friggin' liver. That was low!

Gus and Charlie bought some greasy hamburgers and proceeded to eat the meal of their lives.

Gus: Thanks.

Charlie: No, thank you. You taught me something today.

Gus: Well then, if you want to show your gratitude, let me have some fun in the next chapter.

Charlie: Sorry, Gus I can't let you influence me in that way. Besides, I haven't even figured out what the next chapter will be about.

Gus: That's cool. You can't hurt a guy for trying.

Charlie: Take it easy, Gus.

Gus: Asta la vista, Baby.

Charlie ended the fourth chapter. It was a tough one to write. After revising it approximately 100 times he finally felt good about it. He was also feeling pretty good about Gus. Maybe in the next chapter he'll have Gus grow a few inches and lose the zits. Maybe he'll really have Gus meet the perfect foster family. Maybe he'll even get him laid. Yup, that's exactly what will happen. He'll do all of those things!

Charlie: Hey, who the hell wrote that. Oh Gus.......Gus!!
Gus: Yes, boss.
Charlie: You wrote that paragraph, didn't you?
Gus: Sorry, amigo. It didn't take a genius to break into your computer—but if it did—

Gus woke up and looked down...it was gone!!!!!!!

Gus: Okay, Okay. No more writing without your permission.

Gus woke up and looked down. It was gone!!!!!!!! The large zit on his chin had somehow disappeared. A change for the better, he thought. A change for the better.

References
King, Stephen. Four Past Midnight. New York: Signet Books, 1991.

5. Bedtime, and a Wee Bit More

I am a passenger riding in the front seat of a fast moving car. It's hot outside...I'm sweltering. My exposed skin sticks to the black vinyl. The car reeks of alcohol......and something else......rancid meat. Pieces of it are strewn along the back seat....... like mindless passengers awaiting a second slaughter. I try to roll down the window, but it won't budge. I try again, the handle snaps violently in my hand. The unseen driver laughs and begins singing:

"Frere Jaques, Frere Jaques, dormez-vous?" He stops and cries aloud, "Are you sleeping, Jack? Are you ready for the train?" I scream but no one hears. The car pulls off the road. "The train is comin', Gussy."

I jolt upwards. My t-shirt is soaked. I feel my heart pounding. The digital clock reads 3:08 a.m. Four hours and fifty two minutes until we can get up. Four hours and fifty two friggin minutes until we can get up!

Bedtime sucks when you have a history of being sexually abused. Stimulation, activity, interaction, the great elements and diversions of the day, all cease when you get into bed and the lights are extinguished. Alone and scared, with nothing to occupy your mind, the memories drift back. The bad memories.

For many kids, like me, the beginning of bedtime starts an inexorable journey down the pathway to hell. The demons wait. They coil behind bedposts, lurk in doorways, and masquerade as harmless shadows.

At times, fatigue or pure determination will fight them off. You either drift off or raise a defiant shield: "I won't think about the bad stuff tonight. I won't," you proclaim. Sometimes this works. Sometimes.

But sooner or later the demons will clutch your

61

soul and drag you back. Suddenly, you're there, where it all began. The abuse, that is.

For me, I'm back in my own bed. I can hear my mother's boyfriend, Ronald, swaying up the stairs. Mom's not home—she works the night shift at the post office.

Maybe tonight the drunken bastard will fall and crack his damn neck. But the bedroom door begins to creak open and the profile of a grizzled, pathetic creature of a man, now looms ominously on the bedroom wall. The door stops moving and he begins his approach.

"Gussy-boy, — you awake?"

It doesn't matter whether I pretend to be sleeping.

"The train's headin' for the tunnel, Gussy-boy........choo choo ...choo choo....got to let the train into the tunnel. If it don't.....a boy could get killed."

I figured he meant it. I once saw him shoot a dog. He was mean (not the dog).

It hurt—but I never let on how much. "Choo Choo...train's in real good!" he'd yell. Ronald went at me for three years before I told. Most of us kids have Ronalds in our closets. They never go away...and they come back at night. They like the night.

Occasionally, I'll see him during the daytime. At the mall, in school, or at the gym—it can be anywhere. Something about a stranger will remind me of him. I can be in a great mood, but that reminder will bring me down. I'll remember the pain. When this happens, I can go in any direction. Sometimes, after a painful "association" (as my therapist calls them), I just want to kill, to strike out. On other occasions, I just get down. I'm coming to terms with this. But it's been a struggle.

Kids in residential treatment who have been sexually abused can have bad associations. Occasionally, a new staff member will remind a kid of the jerk who abused him. The kid will usually make life hell for that person. If the kid and that new staff member can work through the shit, if the kid can learn to trust and accept that person who reminds him of the abuser, it usually is a big step forward. I know. I've been the route.

Back to bedtime. No, one more thought (I'm going with my associations—bear with me, I'm still a troubled lad).

I think staff members in residential centers, even the good ones, tend to get too sensitized to abuse. What does that mean, you say? Well, kid after kid enters residential care with a history of being sexually and/or physically abused. We get lumped together. Because we're all alike, people tend to unconsciously minimize what we've experienced. After a short while, we're known more for our problematic behavior than for how badly we were abused—and how that affects us.

Let me make this a little more clear. Remember a few years back, when that little girl fell down a large hole? I forget her name. But the entire country was riveted to news about her condition. Men would come home from work, "Hey, honey, did they get the kid out?" When the girl was finally rescued, the whole country rejoiced. People sent cards, money, goods— they couldn't do enough for this little girl. I think they even had a parade in her honor. Well, EXCUSE ME! All she did was fall down a damn hole and everybody loved her. She had three days of pain, I had three years.

If the entire country, including the staff where I'm living now, could have seen, first hand, what was happening to me, the ensuing sympathy and support would have been unreal. Money and compassion would have flowed: "Hey, Honey, let's send a new bike to that abused kid. Heck, let's give him the car! I still can't believe he survived."

It's crazy.

And what about police brutality? It's out there. But so are a lot of good cops. But when the brutality is caught on videotape—à la Rodney King—the world screams. *Well, who the hell is screaming for us?* Do we need to videotape maggots like Ronald, in the act, to get some attention?

It's easy for staff members to get mad at us. It's even easy for us to get mad at us. We do a lot of provocative acting out. But the behavior comes from somewhere. A staff member once told me that misbehavior is nothing more than a neon light flashing over a kid's head, stating: "I NEED HELP!" "I NEED HELP!" "I NEED HELP!" Not enough people see the light(s).

Howie, one of my favorite child care workers, once told me that when he's totally had it with one of us, he goes down to the record room and reads the kid's history. He says afterwards he feels more compassion and less anger towards the boy. He said he's had to read mine a number of times. Sometimes Howie can be a wuss.

Jesus, this chapter is all over the place. I guess that's what bedtime is all about. Prior to getting into bed, or minutes afterwards, it's not uncommon for a scared kid to "act up" or come up with a "delaying tactic" to avoid the quiet of the night—and the demons.

I couldn't write this "bedtime" chapter without doing the same thing (i.e., delaying, digressing, acting-up). Ain't that interesting? It's not how I planned it.

When I lived on a younger boys unit, bedtime was almost always an event. Take a look:

Ten of us had 9 o'clock bedtimes. Prior to bed, we were kept quiet in front of the T.V. Around 8:40 p.m., one by one, we were sent to the bathroom. Some of us never made it. Getting up from the couch, or from a prone position on the rug, a quick but subtle kick to one of our comrades, would get the ball rolling.

"Gus, please take a time-out. I saw you kick Chris."
"I did not!"
"Gus, please go to the time-out seat."
"But I didn't do anything!! You guys always pick on me!"

Of course I kicked the dude. I had to do something to avoid going to bed. *Ronald was waiting.*

If I really pushed it, it might be 11:00 p.m. before I finally entered my room. And by then, I'd be a lot more tired, maybe from being restrained. Maybe, if I was lucky, I'd fall asleep quickly.

Other kids used other tactics to avoid their Ronalds. Jimmy used the "night light" ploy:

"Staff, my night light won't work. I can't sleep without a night light."

"Staff, Peter broke my night light. I want a night light!"

"Staff, I can't find my night light. Please, I need a night light!"

Peter was equally successful in using the ever popular anti-night light technique:

"Staff, I can't sleep with that light on—it's too bright."
"Staff, tell Jimmy to stop playing with the light!"
"STAFF!! I just burned my finger on the light!"

Mac, he had the uncanny ability to biologically decompensate exactly at 9:00 p.m. He was a master:

"Staff, I have an upset stomach, I just puked in the toilet."
"Staff, I'm itchy all over. Do something."
"Staff, I can't move my bowels!"

Gary used a more psychological approach. He was the "Big Revealer." When the staff member came into his room to say good night, Gary would spring into action:

Staff: *Good night, Gary.*
Gary: *Don't leave. I have something important to talk about.*
Staff: *Can't it wait until tomorrow?*
Gary: *No, I can't tell anyone but you. You're the only one I trust.*

(Gary would use the same line—no matter who was on.)

Staff: *Okay, what is it?*
Gary: *I want to talk about my abuse.*

Gary would make up things or repeat old information over and over. He had the knack for tugging at heart strings. He had great style.

Many kids simply acted-out once they got into bed. John used to throw things from his room. Dave was the spit-ball king. Brucie used to knock on walls.

The staff members hated bedtime almost as much

66

as the kids did. Intellectually, most of them knew why we acted out, about our fears. But, when you're on your twelfth hour and you're tired, knocking on walls and spit-balls piss you off.

Bedtime was also tough on staff for another reason. When you're putting ten troubled kids to bed, you have to be damn careful how much time you spend with each one of them. If a staff member spent ten extra minutes talking to Gary, we all wanted ten extra minutes. There was no way for staff to give us the time and nurturance we all needed. Ideally, each one of us should have had our own staff member sitting with us, assuring us, telling us a bedtime story, whatever it took. But with ten kids and only two staff that wasn't possible. The only way to guarantee extra attention was to act-up or develop a good ploy or tactic.

This is where the reality of group care hits hard. Abused kids need a lot more T. L. C. at bedtime than staff generally have the resources to provide. I would guess some places are better than others. I think the staff members with good hearts are more frustrated at bedtime than at any other time of the day. It's a period in which their hands are tied.

Bedtime is supposed to be a quiet period. Most of the staff go home as the kids go to bed. Agencies can't afford to keep too many people on duty at this time. If they could there would be more compassion.

It's funny. If you asked someone with normal intelligence where would be the best place to treat a troubled kid with behavior problems, the answer would not be: With ten or twelve other kids with similar problems.

Technically, you should put troubled kids with

"normal" kids. They'd get better a lot quicker. Hell can break lose when we're all together. We feed off each other. We learn new ways to act-out from our associates. We learn about self-abuse, physical restraint, and the other 101 ways to act-out we never knew existed. The only reason I can figure that group homes and treatment centers exist as they do is money. It wouldn't be "cost-effective" (I do some calculations for the Hill's Business Manager, Ruth) to have group homes with only two or three kids. The rate the state pays the group home for each kid wouldn't support such a small establishment. According to Ruth, there needs to be eight to 15 kids on a unit to make it financially feasible. That's eight to 15 kids with only two to four staff on duty. It's not enough. Sure, good treatment does occur in residential treatment centers and group homes even with the lousy ratios. I've seen a lot of kids do pretty well here at the Hills. My point is that they'd do even better if the staff-child ratios were better.

I talked about this in the first chapter. The issue of kids wanting attention. Now and then every kid hears the put down: "You're just looking for attention." We're at times made to feel bad about this. But when you live with a dozen other disturbed kids, is it fair to think we're always going to get the attention we deserve? I don't think so! And remember, most of us end up in residential treatment because of abuse and neglect. We never got the attention we deserved. So we need and ask for even more. Why the hell not?

People who work in residential settings for troubled kids need to be aware of certain realities. Here's a Biggie (I figured it out with my therapist, Ellen): The treatment a program offers (i.e., how they talk to kids, what rules they develop, who they take in, and their philosophy, etc.) is very much based on the resources of the program—*not on what is therapeutically ideal.*

Nowhere is this point more evident than at bedtime. (I figured this out on my own.) A scarey, anxious period of the day, common sense would dictate that every program put high numbers of staff on duty to ease this period for the children. But, as mentioned, financial realities don't allow for this. So what happens?

Well, at Highland Hills (my place), if a kid is caught fooling around after bedtime he gets major consequences. He could get three or four hours of time-out the next day, be grounded, and lose certain privileges. Why? Because, the program can't afford to have kids fooling around at night. If other kids got up and there was havoc, there wouldn't be enough staff to handle the situation. Which would threaten the overall safety of the children. Safety—the Big "S"—always comes first. So, bedtime shennanigans are squashed and squashed big.

Now, is this terribly therapeutic? Again, "I don't think so." What *would* be "therapeutic" is five awake staff on duty all night. A kid experiencing nighttime difficulties could be attended to quickly, and appropriately separated, if indicated—without major consequences. This would closer approach the therapeutic ideal.

If staff members better understand how their program's resources influence their treatment techniques, the kids will benefit. If, for instance, a program needs to administer heavy consequences for bedtime problems because of the staffing ratio, an informed worker—aware of the resource issue—might strongly advocate for better staffing patterns. I think new staff members (and probably old ones) don't realize how much their program's lack of resources influence the treatment. They are led to believe that what they do is what is right. Again, I DON'T THINK SO!

Two other things happen at bedtime: Sexual stuff and bedwetting (and are generally exclusive).

At times, kids get sexual at night—particularly the adolescents. Programs, like the Hills, try everything they can to stop this kind of activity, but most, I assume, realize there's only so much they can do.

Think about it. Eight to twelve boys (or girls) are placed in a residential setting for emotionally disturbed kiddos. They are given limited freedom, because the program and society (in this case, represented by the state social service's department) don't trust them (and they shouldn't). After all, each one of us had demonstrated significant behavior problems, often of a sexual nature. (Prior to coming to the Hills, I had this habit of exposing myself on billboards.)

So, we are put away in this "home" for troubled boys where some of us will experience most of our adolescence. We are told to abide by a certain set of rules. We are told sex play is forbidden. We are given limited latitude with the babes, due to liability concerns and distrust. So, what happens when the hormones start to gyrate and the outlets are out of reach? Well, discovering masturbation helps. But, after awhile, your hand gets tired and you yearn for more.

Adding fuel to the fire is, of course, our histories. As I stated in the first chapter, when you've been sexually abused, your hormone switch gets turned on early. Sex is on your mind—a lot.

Someone (the abuser) started something with you and now you feel driven, at times, to finish it off right, to "master" the experience. Yet unfortunately, the finishing, the mastering, which can start shortly after the abuse, may continue for a lifetime—if the right help doesn't come.

In general, we're confused as hell about this sex thing. I think a lot of prostitutes, male and female, were abused as kids, and are now trying to master their hurt by now controlling something (sex) that was forced upon them.

I ran away last year and stayed with three prostitutes in the city. Our histories were dishearteningly similar.

So given all this, I think it's somewhat understandable and predictable that abused kids (boys or girls) living in group care situations are going to get involved sexually with one another. If the home is all boys, then it will be the boys getting it on. Are we homosexual? I think with most of us it's too early to tell. I do think that given the lack of love and intimacy we have all generally experienced, the sexual interactions we have are motivated more by the pain of emptiness and the ramifications of abuse, than any true proclivity towards partners of the same sex. In simple terms, we take it where we can get it.

Now don't get me wrong. I'm not saying it's right that some of us get involved in clandestine sexual liaisons, either with the same or opposite sex. Getting involved, particularly when we're in our early teens, if not younger, often serves to confuse and/or shame

71

us even more. But sometimes the urge is just too great to fight off. I just want you folks to understand this.

Obviously, bedtime is the time where most of this is going to happen. Some kids try to force themselves on others. Some kids are easy targets. This reality adds to the bedtime tension most of us experience. It also adds to staff uneasiness, as well. Some of the staff members, particularly the men, have a real hard time when they catch two boys in the act. They freak.

I would guess seeing two boys fooling around is grossly out of the norm for these staff members. They see it as quite perverted. What some don't understand is that this kind of behavior might be closer to the "norm" for the boys in question.

Because of AIDS, the sex thing has grown even more intense. We all get condoms and lots of education, but the sixty-four thousand dollar question is: Will we heed the advice? Some of us are so angry we don't give a darn if we get it. Some of us, I think, would see getting AIDS as the truest confirmation of our "no good" status. "It figures I got it."

A lot of us just block out the whole thing. After all, many of us have been repeatedly abused in the biblical sense. We might be HIV positive, we may already be doomed. Me, I've avoided getting tested like the plague. Denial, one of my favorite defense mechanisms, sometimes works. Then again, defense mechanisms, from what I've read, are supposed to be unconscious, so maybe I'm getting closer to this issue. Great, another grey cloud over my already dark horizon.

Actually, what really worries me about this AIDS thing is not so much the kids but the staff. It's already hard to work with abused, angry kids. If there isn't enough AIDS training and support for staff members, we could start being treated like lepers. I had this dream (no, nightmare) the other night. I was in the movie "Ben Hur." I was living in the leper colony with Ben's mother and sister. At the end of the movie, when the rain changed them back, I got worse!

All the staff use gloves now when dealing medically with us. I guess this makes sense. Just takes a little time getting used to. But it seems some staff members won't even wipe their own asses without wearing the damn things! If it appears this issue has got me on edge, then the perception is accurate. I'm scared stiff. With my luck, I probably got it.

We were talking about bedtime. Bed-wetting is a pretty common thing. A lot of us kids leak at night. It's nice if the staff members are compassionate about this. Some of us are embarrassed when this occurs. I had a former foster mother who made me wear diapers at night. God, did that suck. Before I left her home, I pissed out the window one day and it hit the mailman. I was in another foster placement within 24 hours. I was a "Special Delivery."

I remember four years ago, Lee, this crazy, scared little kid, was admitted, due to some heavy abuse the kid was takin'. He would wet the bed four or five times a night! He kept the staff up all hours changing his sheets. They were getting worn out (both the staff and the sheets).

After about a week, it was the Unit Director's turn to sleep over. Her name was Ellie, and she was sharp. The kids loved her, but they never got anything past her.

Well, after Lee got up for the second time to have

73

his sheets changed, Ellie got smart. She followed Lee back into his room and observed the fully soaked sheets. She then bent down and rubbed her index finger along the wet fabric. She then raised this finger finger to her mouth.....and tasted. "Doesn't taste like urine to me," she bellowed. Little Lee turned white. The poor kid had been sneaking water into his room and feigning the bed-wetting. He just couldn't go very long without having a staff member in his face. I applauded his ingenuity. I was in the next bedroom. I began to look out for the little guy.

One last thing about bedtime before I either digress again or finish this chapter. Psychotropic medication; little pills administered at night to help us sleep.

I've overheard staff members talking about the pills the shrinks put us on. Some staff don't like the idea we take anything. I think it's an "ego" thing. I think they want us to improve the "old fashioned way," through hard work and perseverance. It's the American way!

Fooey! It seems like a lot of us are helped by these medications. They don't cure us, but they seem to help us do the work we need to do, or get to sleep with less difficulty.

Some kids are resistant to go on meds. They've heard a lot of weird things about them. Some kids also have parents with misconceptions or downright mistrust of meds. They discourage or simply don't allow their kid to take the pills. I think this is a damn shame. The pain at bedtime can be unreal. If there's a safe way of easing the agony, I say, "Go for it." It worked for me. I used to take an anti-depressant, desipramine. It helped. And there were no side effects.

Well, I think I've said as much as I can about bedtime, and, I guess, a wee bit more. Some kids can handle it—some can't. It has the potential to be a real "nightmare." Staff members need a lot of support to support us at night. I hope they get it.

The car is traveling down the same familiar road. Everything outside appears grey and motionless. Inside, the air is stifling. The driver's eyes are fixated on the road ahead. His breath smells of bourbon, his haggard face wears a baleful signature. His foot presses gingerly on the accelerator, thrusting the six cylinder vehicle ominously ahead. My heart pounds in excruciating rhythm. I gasp for air as my lungs begin to panic. Suddenly, the driver jerks the wheel to the right, and the treadless white walls connect with a dirt road that lay hidden underneath the branches of a large pine. "We're almost there, Gussy-boy...... trains revving up.....Oh, momma, I can feel the heat of the engine." Abruptly, the car skids to a stop. The driver turns to me and reveals a grotesque, almost toothless grin. "Get the tunnel ready, Gussy-boy" he now taunts as his hands begin to undo his tattered trousers. "NOT THIS TIME, SCUM BAG!" I cry out with vengeful ecstasy. With all the force my abused frame can muster, I drive my fist into the monster's piteous face, feeling the shattered particles of his nose scatter beneath my penetrating flesh. A scream pierces the air as he grabs for his wounded feature. I lurch again and deliver one more mammoth blow to his face.....it knocks his fuckin' head right off his body. "Holy shit!" I proclaim.

Suddenly a large hand grasps my shoulder. I jolt upwards.

"Are you okay, Gus? You were doing a lot of tossing and turning in your bed...another nightmare?"

"I'm all right. Thanks."

I lower my head to the pillow as a small smile crosses my lips.

I beat him...tonight.

6. Friendship

Everyone needs friends. Friends get you through hard times. Friends make you laugh. Friends give you weggies. Friends loan you money. Friends care about you.

When I first got to the Hills, four years ago, I had never had a best friend. There are lots of us who come here never having connected with another kid. This sucks. We wear this failure like a neon light on a black wall.

Two years ago, Bobby and I snuck down to the kitchen after tuck-in and pigged out on some cold chili. Man, we farted all night. God, did we laugh. I'll never forget that night. Bobby was my first buddy.

Abused and neglected kids need to take care of themselves first—before they can worry about some-one else's needs. It's a full-time job. When I lived at home I worried about getting fed, having enough clothes, not getting beaten, my mother's drinking, sexual abuse, and whether the heat would come on. I was so preoccupied with my own stuff I never had time to worry about anything else. I spent most of my time trying to survive. Sometimes, I worried about disappearing. Life was awful. I never laughed much.

The professionals used terms to describe me like "egocentric" and "narcissistic." I had one idiot social worker who used to talk about me—in front of me—as if I wasn't there. I hate when people do that! At first, I didn't know what the two terms mean (ego-centric and narcissistic).

"Maybe they mean I'm unique and special," I queried. I was in for a rude awakening.

Unfortunately, it turned out, I was far from unique. When I got to the Hills, I noticed that most of the kids were just like me, into themselves and socially underdeveloped. I noticed one other thing. We all suffered because of this. Suffered terribly.

One day I was getting picked on by Carl Spooner. Carl was big and crazy. I was scared of that boy, and he knew it. On this particular day, Carl was making fun of my weight. I was on the verge of tears. Well, Bobby happens to stroll in from a home visit, just as Carl was really letting me have it. Before you can say, "Holy tomatoes," Bobby runs at Carl and grabs a chunk of his hair and proceeds to bite his nose. I never heard a kid yell so loud. Two staff members had to pull Bobby off him. Carl seemed in shock. He had been out-crazed. The bastard never bothered me again. No kid had ever stuck up for me like Bobby did that day. I'll never forget it. Never.

Most of us come in to group care lonely and hungry to relate. But we have lousy table manners—if you catch my drift. One day we're buddy-buddy with a kid, the next day we're fighting. *Nothing ever gets sustained.*

Once, when I was hanging out in the library—I had a crush on Latisha Watkins, the 29 year old librarian—I scanned a few books on developmental psychology and peer relations. One, written by a dude named Sullivan, talked about how important it was (is) for a young child to develop his/her first best friend.

Actually, I think he used the term "chum". I think he was referring to kids between five and twelve years old.

According to Ol' Sully, when a kid makes his first best friend, he has to give up some of his selfishness and, yes, egocentrism (my thing) in order to enjoy and sustain the friendship. He learns about and experiences the normal "give and take" of a sustained relationship. Around five, peer relations become very important and energizing. Instead of having all his/her needs met by Mommy or Daddy, the fivish dude looks to his/her friends to meet key needs. It's a developmental thing. According to the theory, it feels so good to have a best friend a kid will readily relinquish his or her egocentrism (there's that term, again).

Bobby and I used to count our pubic hairs. At first, we used a magnifying glass. I remember one time using the glass outside. God, I almost burnt it off!

As a walking and talking little dude, the typical five year old—if I understand the literature correctly—must emotionally separate from his folks and learn to fend for himself, with the support of his pals.

The kid becomes a real little person. If he's too into himself ("me", "me", "me"), due to certain primitive needs never being met, and can't get along with the other kids (or teachers), he's gonna be in heavy you-know-what, according to the theorists.

Well, folks, Sully and the others were on to something. I got plastered when I hit first grade. Developmentally, I was light years behind the others. The pain of not fitting in and getting teased was unreal. I hated going to school. I felt like a misfit. I often tantrummed at breakfast, hoping to be kept home. I knew most of the kids didn't like me. I knew they talked behind my back. I even became a little paranoid. And there was nothing I could do. I simply wasn't ready for the "give and take."

When it came to getting along, I simply couldn't put anyone else's needs ahead of my own. *Looking out for number one was all I knew.* My mother had consistently failed to do this, so it was my job—and I did it with gusto!! As a result, I got in tons of fights. I was picked on, scapegoated, and bounced from two public schools. (I couldn't believe it when the Angier school expelled me for throwing a kid's coat on the ground and stepping on it! How the hell did I know the kid was still in it?)

Bobby had burn marks on his arm. He never talked about them. I don't think they got there by "accident." The better I got to know Bobby, the more those marks bothered me.

You see, little humanoids like me (the abused and neglected kind) don't necessarily act out because of what happened to us. No, we often "act-out" because the abuse and neglect caused serious ramifications— like not being able to make and sustain a goddamn friendship because we're too "me, me, me."

Bobby was discharged from the program eight months ago. I really miss him. When I was with him, I felt cool. I felt "in." I felt connected. Life was easier and more fun after hooking up with old Bobby. I don't hear from him much anymore. He's getting on with his life. Carl's still here, and he's got this little scar on his nose. I won't forget Bobby.

As I've pointed out, making friends is crucial to our development. Yet kids like me are often unprepared to do so. Socially, we're often like bulls in a china shop. (You know, I don't think I've ever seen a china shop. What the hell is a china shop?)

A new kid, Marcus, came to the Hills a few months ago. He has to be in control of everything and he's a real know-it-all. None of the kids like him. He won't say it, but he's hurtin' inside. He's lonely. I know, I was there.

So, how does residential treatment help us to improve our social skills? Develop some buddies? Move ahead developmentally? Some programs, I think, help more than others. I guess it depends on how serious they take it. How much they understand the importance of friendship building.

Group homes and places like the Hills are often loud and chaotic. I think it feels good to everyone when there's not much acting out and things are relatively quiet. But, there's the rub, amigos.

Sometimes, friendship building (a necessary developmental-type thing) is sacrificed, or simply not prioritized, because the agency lacks the resources to facilitate enhanced peer interactions or simply because the agency does not place enough value on this aspect of milieu therapy. Some agencies which do not emphasize friendship building in and/or outside their

81

program do so because the process can be, at times, potentially disruptive. For instance, say two kids are arguing over something. To "quiet" the situation, a staff member might intervene and quickly settle the matter. This intervention would keep the "lid on" (a popular term in the residential world). Yet this intervention would not help the two children in question learn to settle their differences.

One day, Marcus is going to find a best friend. It will be an intoxicating experience. He'll feel great. There's nothing like a best friend—especially your first one. I think everyone remembers his/her first "best" friend.

Staff members in places, like the Hills, generally don't want a whole lot of acting-out, disruptive behavior from the kiddos. And who can blame them? We're tough! It's hard just getting through a typical, "routine" day. So sometimes, staff act in ways which serve their needs more than the needs of the kids. It's often a necessary evil. Sometimes they just don't have the training, time and/or energy to promote and facilitate healthier peer relations.

Last year I ran away with three kids because they were the three "coolest" kids at the Hills. I didn't want to run away. But it felt great to be asked by them, to be accepted. At the time, I wasn't feeling very good about myself.

Here at the Hills, they're trying something new with respect to helping kids improve socialization skills (i.e., make friends). They call it "Duo Therapy." It's cool. One therapist sees two kids at once. Most of the kids in the duos are kids who have trouble getting along. It seems like it's working. Carl, the bully, was matched with Andrew. They couldn't be more different. Carl's loud and bossy; Andrew's quiet and meek. Yet they seem to be hitting it off. I heard Andrew tell Carl to "Shut up and listen" the other day. I was shocked. I thought Carl would deck him. At first, it looked like he would. You could see it in his eyes. But he paused, and then, to my amazement, he shut up and listened. The two are becoming friends; Carl didn't want to blow it.

Friendship; it's powerful.

My roomate Hector is currently my best friend. We talk a lot about girls and doing it. We also sneak in cigarettes from time to time. I sometimes hear Hector crying at night. He really misses his family, but remembers the pain. Sometimes, to help him, I'll sit next to his bed and read a book out loud. He also helps me when I'm down. We need each other. We're important to each other. Although we're both hurtin', there's a joy in what we have together.

7. Mom's Perspective

The letter was on my bed when I got home. It was thick. At first, I didn't know who it was from. But as I got closer to the bed, the scribbled penmanship startled this scrabbled brain. Mother. She was making contact. Again.

Nervously, I opened the letter. A bead of sweat formed and departed from my brow. My heart raced. And that old knot that never goes too far returned to my stomach. Mother. A word synonomous with every known adjective, including all expletives deleted, was now resonating in my brain. Mother.

"What did she want?" "What's it gonna be this time?" Hope. Despair. Anger. Loneliness. My hands shook as my contorting brain tried to begin the process of reading. "Jesus, she's written me a friggin' book..."

Slowly, I lowered my butt to the mattress, kicked off my shoes, and began to read...

Dear Gus,

It's been almost six months since I last saw you. I'm living in a small town in Vermont named Castle Stone. I'm staying with a friend, Bonnie. She and I used to waitress together at the White Horse. She's got a small house on a pretty little lake. I'm working the night shift at the local post office. I haven't had a drink in four months. I go to AA meetings twice a week. For the first time in a long time, I'm feeling good.

I know. You've heard this all before. And maybe this time won't be any different...but maybe it will. Look, kid, I don't expect you to have much faith left in your old mom—especially after the last go round. But there are things I want you to know, feelings I want to share. Please, Gus, read this entire letter, and then think what you want. It's important. I'm going to tell you things I've never had the courage to share. And please, don't send this letter back with the grammar corrected. I hate when you do that! You know, it can be somewhat intimidating having a genius for a son.

O.K., let's start with a recap.

You don't see me for five years and then, one day, I'm at the Hills and want to get you back. We start visiting and going to therapy together and then, one day, they start talking about you coming home—for good. Well, you know the rest. I begin drinking again. I screw up at work. I don't show up for a number of home visits, and then, one day, I'm history—again. The Big "D". The Big Disappointer, that's me.

Gus, you have every reason to hate me. I've set you up more times than I want to remember. But for what it's worth, I want to do some explaining. If it doesn't help you, at least it will help me.

I really wanted us to be a family again. But I freaked. Thinking about being a parent to an adolescent. Thinking about making decisions. Thinking about doing it right. It became overwhelming. I thought I was ready. But I wasn't. And living in that new town, not knowing anyone, that didn't help. I guess I could have used more support. But I didn't know how to get it. So, I turned to the bottle, the wrong kind of support.

Gus, I've told you about my childhood, but I never told you everything. Thinking back, I don't have many pleasant memories. Hell, for most of my adult life, I've tried to keep my past blocked away.

But lately, with the help of my new therapist, Marge, I've (we've) been doing a lot of digging. She thinks it might be helpful for you to hear where I've been. To really hear.

I told you that I was sexually abused by my mother's brother for almost seven years. I told you how he threatened to kill me if I told. But I never talked to you much about my mother. I loved her. And I hated her. She should have protected me. When she finally found out about the abuse she denied that it happened. She said she would have known. She knew.

My mother never wanted me. And I don't think she ever let me forget it. According to mom, there were four guys who could have been my father. Two of them were strangers—one night standeroos. She was supposed to get an abortion, but got smashed the day before the procedure and was too hung over to get it done. After that, she fell in love with a new guy who wasn't too thrilled about her being pregnant. As soon as I was born, he took off. My mother was still a teenager when I came out. She was more into partying than mothering. During my first four years I was bounced from relative to relative. I didn't stay in one place for very long.

In case you're wondering, I found out a lot of this information from my Aunt Helen. She's still living in Waltham, Massachusetts. As you know, Helen has always been my "old reliable." The only person I could ever truly count on. Lately, we've been writing and talking on the phone. She's been helping me put the pieces together.

Anyways, at four my mother took me back (the welfare payments enticed her). From what I can remember, we actually had some O.K. years. I mean, no one got hurt and we actually stayed in the same place for awhile. I remember that my mother never really treated me as a daughter— more like a peer, a roommate. I thought that was how all mothers treated their daughters. I didn't realize how disastrous this was until very recently. Until I began working with my therapist, Marge.

I guess I lost—or never had the opportunity—to be a little kid. I was too worried. I had to look out for my mother. I had big responsibilities. While all the other kids were playing house I was keeping it. As a result, I lost something. I lost what all the other kids got. The privilege to experience the world through the eyes of a little girl. To receive the emotional juices that flow to all such aspiring young Barbies. To be a healthy adult, it sure helps if you had a healthy childhood. Well, pal, I didn't. And, I guess, neither have you. I still mourn my lost childhood.

I can see now that how I treated you was very similar to how I got treated. I'm sorry about this. I never realized what was going on. I was simply doing the best I could with what I had, which wasn't much, and wasn't enough.

Actually the whole thing is kind of ironic. Because I had to be more "grown-up" as a little girl, I ended up being more immature as I got older. In fact, as a teenager (and, at times, as an adult) I've often acted just like a bratty little twit; obnoxious, impulsive, loud, and unruly. All the behaviors I never got to unleash when I lived with my mother, when those behaviors would have appeared somewhat "normal." Of course, the sexual abuse didn't help, either.

Uncle Billy came to live with us when I was seven. He had a good job with the Gas company. He helped my mother with the bills. He also helped himself to me. He was an alcoholic. And he was scary. You never could predict what he'd say or do. Once, after getting into an argument with his boss, he came home and beat the hell out of my mother and me. She pleaded with me not to tell anyone what happened. She had become dependent on Uncle Billy. The needlemarks on her arms, which she called "hives," I guess made her very dependent. Years later, she spoke to me about her "heroin" period (after I got busted shooting the same crap).

Not long after Uncle Billy moved in, he started coming on to me. At first, it was through compliments. "My, my, doesn't our little girl look pretty today." "Jesus, just look at our little Mary. The boys will be fighting all day over you." At first, I kind of liked the attention. I wasn't used to receiving praise. I never thought I was pretty. No one ever told me I was. Well, Aunt Helen always made me feel special, but I didn't see her too much. So, it was nice to hear Uncle Billy say such things.

But soon the words no longer felt good. It was his eyes that changed them. He'd say the same things but would stare right through me. His eyes told me something wasn't right. I began to avoid him. Then, one night, when my mother was out—she was a waitress at the local dive—he came into my room and raped me. I was only seven. The pain was unbearable. And he smelled something awful. Afterwards, he returned with a large, shiny hunting knife. He told me, specifically, where he would cut if I ever told. I never did, until I ran away seven years later.

Uncle Billy lived with us, on and off, for *seven* years. And he was on and off me for all that time. I never told anybody. Not even my friends—the few I had. So many times I wanted to tell my mother. But she was so weak and he was so threatening. I hated her for bringing this man into our home. Even though it hadn't been perfect, the three years I lived alone with her, from four to seven, were probably the three best of my childhood.

Gus, I wanted so desperately for my mother to love me, to save me—but it never came out right. She was a very nervous woman with a terrible self-image. I know that now. Whenever the pressure got too much, she turned to the bottle or the drugs. Only now do I realize how hurtin' she really was. I spent a lot of my youth getting her to bed and dressed for work. Her quiet appreciation of my usefulness seemed to sustain me. But that's a pretty shitty way to get raised.

At fourteen, I ran away from home. I couldn't take it anymore. I stayed with Molly O'Hara, the one true friend I had. Molly eventually told her parents why I had run off and they called the police. I was put in a temporary foster home while an investigation was conducted. Uncle Billy, at first, denied everything, and mom supported him. She refused to believe me.

Billy eventually admitted the abuse and copped a plea. According to my Aunt Helen (who knows everything), Billy kind of cracked up in front of one of the investigators. Apparently, he started screaming, "No grandpa! No grandpa!"

It turns out both Billy and my mother were sexually molested by their mother's dad. A nice legacy, eh?

Billy got probation and was ordered to attend therapy sessions, as well as weekly AA meetings. He was also restricted from being near me.

With Billy out of the house, I was returned home. I was also hooked up with a therapist from the local mental health clinic.

The first thing my mother said when I came home was, "You happy 'bout what you've done?" "What I did!" I screamed. "That bastard fucked me for seven years and you did NOTHING. What I'VE done?" I stormed out of the house and ran to the clinic. Ann, my therapist, sat with me as I cried for forty-five minutes. She then called my mother who reluctantly joined us. It was the first time I had ever seen my mother cry, for me.

Ann was beautiful. She was very patient and warm towards my mother. She let her blow off steam by putting me down before, somehow, she got my mother to fess up. All of a sudden, my mother is bawlin' her eyes out and asking God to forgive her. Over the next six months, Ann, my mother, and I had some amazing sessions. At one point, my mother claimed she was furious with me for letting the abuse go on without me saying anything. When Ann pressed her about this, she was able, with Ann's help, to see that much of her anger was due to *her* inability to say anything when *she* had been repeatedly molested. She also revealed how guilty she had felt for remaining quiet about Uncle Billy. She had a "feeling" something was going on.

Six months into the treatment, Ann left the clinic. Mom and I were devastated. We loved that lady. The new therapist, Rebecca,was not our cup of tea. After a few months, we both stopped showin' up. A few months later, Mom was drinking heavily again and we began having humongous arguments.

Around that time, I was about 15 or 16, I started drinking and getting laid by any guy who smiled at me. I felt like such a piece of shit, I was so empty, that sex—with any guy who wanted me—would fill a need. I made some awful decisions in those days. My mother, at times, even tried to discipline me—something she was not too familiar doing. But my rage and her guilt left mom pretty much ineffective. Sadly, mom was always more comfortable treating me like a peer than a daughter.

At 18, I got hooked on heroin and was ordered to a drug clinic. I knew my mother had been into heroin. I guess I

91

wanted to follow in her footsteps. When a kid acts like one of his or her parents—even in a bad way—it makes that kid feel closer to the parent. That's what I think. And I've had a lot of time to think about this stuff. By doing heroin, I was identifying with my old lady. And ain't identifying a form of flattery?

Of course, acting-out also helps kids get back at their parents for screwing them over.

I think when kids have been injured by their parents, they go through life continually looking to heal the wounds. Sometimes, the healing can take place even if the parents aren't around any more. Sometimes, the attempt to heal is misguided, like when it involves copying a destructive behavior.

Up until now, I've told you very little about your father. I told you that I hardly knew him. I deflected your attempts to press me for more information. I had my reasons. Let me now fill in some of the pieces for you.

At the drug clinic, I met and fell in love with your father. His name was Fritz Studelmeyer. He had entered the clinic a few weeks before I got there. He was an amazing guy. He could multiply three-digit numbers by three-digit numbers in his head as quick as a calculator. He could also speak fluent Chinese. He learned it while bussing at a Chinese restaurant. When no one was looking, Fritz would call the local Chinese laundry and complain, in Chinese, about them using too much starch. He was a funny guy. He was also very depressed. His moods could turn on a dime. I got pregnant with you while Fritz and I were at the clinic. I thought he was the greatest guy I had ever met.

We were both discharged at the same time. Two weeks later we got married. I was really happy. For the first time in a long time, I was clean and looking forward to the future. Fritz got a job at Radio Shack and I began wait essing. We lived with his older brother, Ziggy.

Well, one day I'm at work and the phone rings. It's the hospital, it's for me. Fritz is dead. Heroin overdose. I freak out and spend two weeks in the psycho ward at the local hospital. My mother visits me once. She couldn't handle my depression, probably because she couldn't handle her own. Luckily, Aunt Helen came forward and offered to let me stay with her after the two weeks were up.

After a few months with Helen, I returned home to live with my mother. Helen really didn't have the room. As I've stated, my mother never really wanted me, therefore, she wasn't too thrilled with you sitting in my growing belly. We fought a lot. But, occasionally, we shared some n ce moments. Mom recounted her fight with drug addiction and we drew, I think, a little closer to one another, even though the fighting continued.

Then, I met Ronald.

I was six months pregnant at the time. He wasn't much to look at. He was an alcoholic. But, he was a way out. I couldn't stay with my mother any longer. The tension was becoming unbearable.

Ronald was my meal ticket. He had inherited his parents' home and made a decent living doing odd jobs and collecting trash. He didn't seem to mind me being pregnant, either. So, I moved in with him and had you.

At first, the beatings weren't so bad. He'd use an open hand. Later, the bastard used his fists. I should have taken you and left the first time he hurt me. But I didn't. I thought at the time I deserved the beatings. He was always complaining about dinner being late, me being too fat, or "that fuckin' kid crying again." I figured he was right on all accounts. Uncle Billy used to beat me, I figured most men

93

were that way. I figured most girls deserved it.

I knew I was no prize. Oddly, the situation was familiar—if not comfortable—to me. That's how I was raised.

Gus, it's taken me a long time, and a lot of therapy and reading, to see how screwed up I was. No one deserves to be abused. No one! Up until now I've denied abusing you sexually. I've refused to talk about it. I wouldn't let your therapist at the Hills get near the subject. I know my "denial," as it's been called, has hurt you even more. I'm sorry.

Sadly and tragically, you were abused, by Ronald—and by me. The longer I stayed with Ronald, the more I coped by drinking and doing cocaine. When you were five, I got fired by the post office for coming in loaded. I "celebrated" my firing by getting even more wasted. And it was in that crazy state that I did things to you, sexual things, with Ronald, that I will regret forever. I don't know how it happened. I don't even know why. I don't remember everything. But I remember enough. I do recall throwing up the next morning—and not because of the booze.

For one brief, repugnant moment which will torture me as long as I live, I became my Uncle Billy. I wore the other shoe. I did to you what had been done to me. And in that moment it had felt good. And that's sick. My therapist, Marge, is helping me sort this stuff out. She's helping me to understand how it could have happened.

Look, Gus, a bad history doesn't take someone off the hook in terms of being responsible for his/her actions, so I'm not going to ask for your forgiveness. Just perhaps for a little understanding, so we can move on. Marge says we've got to put our memories, our pain, in perspective. What's the alternative?

Dammit, Gus, I am so sorry for all of this...and what that monster did to you. When I woke the next morning, I couldn't

94

even look myself in the mirror. I confronted Ronald, and that's when I found out he had been sexually abusing you for three goddamn years. THREE GODDAMN YEARS! What you must have gone through.

I pulled you out of that house as quick as I could. I had nowhere to go but back to my mother's. She had just married Barney. He was actually a good guy, and good for my mother. He worked part time at the local hardware store. He also collected disability payments from the government. While serving in the Army, a jeep ran over his foot and crushed his heel. He still walked with a noticeable limp. Barney was an alcoholic, but had been sober for four years.

I'm sure you remember old Barney. At first, the two of you hit it off pretty good.

When my mother heard what happened, she called yours truly every name under the sun. Barney had to physically restrain her—she wanted to kill me. She then kicked me out of the house. She said I wasn't fit to be a mother. Man, wasn't that the pot calling the kettle black? But how could I argue? Even though I had been drunk out of my gord, I had sexually abused you. I had also failed to protect you for three goddamn years while Ronald did his thing.

Mom insisted that I give up custody of you. She threatened to have me and Ronald prosecuted if I didn't. I hated her for that. She was sticking up for you. She had never stuck up for me. I was enraged, but my guilt and remorse inhibited me from fighting. I simply faded. I signed over your custody to my mother, and let Barney and her raise you.

Gus, I know you've said you don't like to talk much about those years, when you bounced from me, to my mother, to numerous foster homes, and finally were placed at the Hills. I know they weren't easy for you. They weren't easy years for me, either.

I hated visiting you when you lived with my mother. She never let me forget what Ronald and I had done to you. I felt like a piece of crap every time I walked through the door. Heck, maybe she had every right to treat me that way. But who the hell was she? Uncle Billy went at me for seven years, and she did nothing! Who was <u>she</u> to cast stones? Barney tried to get her to lighten up, but she never changed. I think she saw raising you as a way to make up for the mistakes she made with me. This time she'd get it right. Wrong.

My mother wasn't emotionally equipped to raise you—even with Barney's help. I know you lasted two years with them, but don't blame yourself for the acting-out that caused your removal to foster care. You simply had too much to deal with. God, what an awful time that must have been for you.

When you were seven and ordered into foster care, I moved out of state. I couldn't bear to see you being raised by strangers. Strangers that would look at me funny every time I'd come to visit you. I may have been screwed up, but I wasn't stupid. I knew what they'd probably be thinking every time I showed up:

"So that's Gus's mother, the one that sexually abused him."

"Here comes the ex-addict to visit her son."

"What kind of mother abuses her own kid?"

"What kind of mother lets another person abuse her kid for 3 years?"

"Can we trust this woman not to hurt her kid, again?"

"Is she drunk?"

Foster care is supposed to be a "temporary" thing, but I had heard that some foster parents get down right possessive about "their" kids and turn their noses up at the biological parents. I wasn't ready to deal with that.

I was ashamed of who I was, who I had become. And I was angry. I didn't deserve all the crap I was getting. If life had been different for me I would surely have been different. Anyways, I just fled. I ran away from everything. You, my mother, the memories. I had to get away. But as you know, you really can't get away from this stuff. At some point, the music stops and you have to deal with t.

In Maine, where I landed, I made a lot of bad decisions. Life really sucked. I couldn't forget you, my mother, the abuse (mine, as well as yours), that scum-bag Ronald. My brain seemed haunted by the evil from my past.

For the first few years in Maine, I drifted from job to job and increasingly turned to booze to fight off the demons. Then, when money got scarce, I became a two-bit criminal. A little shoplifting here, a little burglary there. I think I wanted to get caught, wanted to be punished. I hated myself. It was a chore getting up in the morning—sometimes I didn't. Life was dark and grey. The days dragged on and the hole I was digging grew wider and deeper. Finally, mercifully, I got caught trying to pass some phony checks. I was sent to the Women's State Penitentiary for 18 months.

It was awful. But, as they say, it turned out to be a "sobering" experience. While in lock-up, I met Claire LaFrancois. She was a guard stationed in my cell block. She actually cared about us. She treated the inmates like real people. She helped me get my act back together.

She, too, had been sexually abused as a kid. We would talk about the ramifications of this. She related a lot of what she and her therapist had worked on together. Sometimes we'd just look at each other and cry. I wish we could have spent more time together. I was lucky to have gotten anything at all.

For the very first time, I started to think it wasn't all my fault. Ann, my former therapist, had tried to work with me on this. But hearing from someone else who had been sexually abused, who had struggled with the very same issues, helped—helped a lot. Claire said that the prison was full of women who had been sexually abused. It was true. People have no idea how prevalent sexual abuse is. But the other thing she said which made a lot of sense was that in homes where there is sexual abuse, there's a higher probability of general dysfunction. In other words, it isn't just the sexual abuse that screws kids up. It's the abuse coupled with in-adequate parenting. The prisons, according to Claire, are full of little souls crying out for their mommies to love them better, and who act out because the love never came (never comes), or wasn't (isn't) enough.

I think having a good childhood is like having a nice foundation for a home. Without a strong foundation you can't build much higher. If you do, it's at risk to crumble. Gus, I've crumbled more times than I'd like to remember. Yet I think I can go higher, and think I am. I'm really work-ing to understand my past without blaming myself or my mother. When you stop the blaming the picture becomes more clear. I think that through understanding and support, abused people like me (like us) get our foundations in place and we grow stronger.

In prison, I thought a lot about you. I decided that I would get you back. Claire helped me to believe that I could. When I got out, I moved closer to you, got a job, began attending AA meetings, and then, after six months, I called Highland Hills. "Hello, Hills, this is Gus's mother, I want my kid back!" It took another four months before I was allowed to visit. Red tape. You gotta love it. The state had custody of you. A good bit of legal maneuvering had to take place before yours truly could begin visiting. At last, I got the green light —and I was one scared momma.

As you are well aware, things started out pretty good. Even though I had not seen you for five years, you were ready to give me a shot. Sure, it was awkward at first, but we seemed to work through the "getting to know you again" jitters.

I hated coming to pick you up. Even though the staff that worked with you all seemed pretty nice, I wondered what they were thinking. It was made pretty clear to me that if I hadn't shown up you would have been matched with a new foster family. I think they even had one picked out and ready to go. Even though she tried to hide it, I think your therapist, Ellen, was upset that I had returned. I'm sure she wasn't alone. Christ, I proved them right! I let you down—again. It got too damn scary.

It was hard picking you up at the Hills. Every time I drove into the driveway, that big sign—**Highland Hills Children's Home**—spoke to me. It said, "Welcome, you failure!" Everybody inside was so good and pure—I was a bum. A parent who had abused her only son. Sometimes, I'd see that sign and want to puke.

The staff that worked with you were very nice. Even though I never spent more than fifteen to twenty minutes in your cottage, I had the sense that the people taking care of you were all pretty caring. Yet I didn't trust any of them. After being jacked around so many times by social workers, lawyers, therapists, etc., etc., I didn't trust anyone. You trust these people, confide in them, and then they leave— or stab you in the back. I have been disappointed more times than I want to remember.

And, boy, was I jealous. I saw how you looked at Ellen. I heard about all the sports you were doing with Neil. I saw your photo album. I longed to be one of those adults you had come to love and admire. I was jealous of them, and their skills. They all seemed so confident. They didn't lose their cool during emergencies, had tons of energy, and knew which words to utter when a kid was down.

Some of the staff talked to me like I was an idiot. Like I had an I.Q. of 65. I think some of the child care workers were simply uncomfortable dealing with the parents. I think it was more fun, for some of them, when we weren't around.

It was also hard coming to the Hills because of what it provided. Beautiful grounds, lots of sports equipment, computers, T.V.'s, nintendos, nice furniture. Gus, I was jealous! You had it better than me! I never had any of that stuff. I never got the kind of clothes they gave you. I never ate as well. I never had a chance to take horseback riding lessons or attend summer camp. I never had people taking care of me who weren't either abusive or alcoholic (or both). Seeing how much you had reminded me of how much I hadn't. Damn it! Why me? Why had life been so fucking awful? Was it all my fault? Claire said it wasn't, but...

You know, when I think about it, that place you live at, Highland Hills, it's like an upper-middle class institution. The furniture, the grounds, the clothes they buy for you—most parents of kids living there can't afford to give their kids the same kind of things! Most of us have trouble making ends meet. Some of us are on welfare. A lot of us don't have what you would consider high-paying jobs. Look, I know the psychological mumbo-jumbo that goes on in group homes and treatment centers is important. Yes, I'm sure it's important for you and for me to talk about our mothers. But for Christ's sakes, Gus, "tangible" help doesn't hurt, either.

Instead of just talking to a parent, how about helping

them find and afford a better apartment? Instead of trying to bring us along therapeutically, how about occasionally bringing us to the grocery store or dentist's office? A lot of us don't have cars. Instead of getting upset if we can't make it in for a therapy session, how about offerring to conduct sessions at *our* house? Instead of trying to get us into a new therapy group, how about trying to help us with membership at the local "Y"?

Talking about problems can certainly help, but sometimes people can be helped more by actions. Heck, don't actions speak louder than words?

Obviously, entering the Hills brought up a lot of stuff for me. In fact, I'm only beginning to sort out how much. Like I said, my new therapist, Marge, is helping a lot. I think, sometimes when I missed visits with you or treated you unfairly, it had to do with my own anger at my own life. I would take it out on you. Jesus, Gus, I'm sorry, honey. I do love you. It kills me that I've caused you so much pain. It wouldn't surprise me if you never wanted to see me again. But I'm not gonna quit on you! The picture of our lives is more clear. I'm finally seeing it with some clarity. Marge is good. I'm not as angry as I once was, nor as brittle. But I still have a long way to go.

Interestingly, I got a package from your therapist, Ellen, last month. In it was a nice letter and information about changes they're making at the Hills. It was good to hear from her. I wasn't sure how she felt about me. I know she couldn't have been too happy about my failure to make it with you. She put a lot of effort into helping us.

Anyways, Ellen talked about exciting changes at the Hills. She said the program was moving ahead, changing from being "kid-centered" to "family-centered." A guide the agencyle put together explained what this meant. It really

101

home. It spoke about many of the things I just mentioned.

I guess, according to what they sent, when residential treatment was first offered to abused and neglected kids forty or fifty years ago, the idea was to work primarily with the kid. Group homes and residential treatment centers took in emotionally disturbed kids, fixed 'em up and then sent them home. Not too much attention was given to the parents. Well, I guess the results weren't terribly impressive. It didn't seem to matter how well a kid was doing at the time of discharge if he or she was returned to a family that hadn't changed too much. If the family hadn't changed, the kid usually ended up out of the home again, usually in worse shape. Big surprise!

So, places like the Hills are now getting smart and going family crazy. I like it. When I was young, my family needed help a lot more than I did.

According to Ellen, the Hills will be looking to form "partnerships" with each child's family. They want parents to spend big chunks of time at the agency, hanging out where their kid is living. She mentioned something about relaxing the boundaries, involving parents in all aspects of their kid's treatment. She said they've started to do this and the results have been great.

I guess at the Hills, you now have parents and siblings coming in and interacting as welcomed, integral members of the residential community. She talked about one mother who makes a mean pizza, and a father who's been dazzling the kids with his basketball wizardry.

The Halloween party sounded like a gas, as well. Parents, siblings, Big Brothers and Sisters, and staff all dressing up together and having one giant party. Right on, Hills! That's the way it should be. I remember walking into that place and feeling low. As nice as people were, I often felt like they were talking down to me. They were the "good guys" and I was the "bad" parent. I used to think: "The hell with them, I'm not such a shit. Get to really know me and you'll see." But other than receiving standard therapy, and the brief "Hello, how ya doing?" there was no opportunity to get to know the people who were taking care of you.

Yet, to be honest, it must be scary as hell for parents to get so involved. I mean, we're always being judged and evaluated. Forget to dot an "i" and everyone wants our kid to stay in treatment another six months. I would think most parents, including this lady, would be nervous as heck about interacting so much with the enemy, I mean the people in "control." 'Cause let's face it, as much as parents and staff become buddy-buddy, they're still the ones in control. They seem to have the weight.

Parents like yours truly, we've usually been in the "system" a very long time. We're not used to having much of a voice. We're used to being told what to do. We're a little wary of authority.

The changes they're making at the Hills. They're good—but make me nervous. They involve parents really needing to trust the Hills' staff. Trust. A word that's disappeared from some of our vocabularies. But heck, I think they re going in the right direction.

Gus, if you feel like writing back, I'd like to hear how this parents stuff is going.

Well, kiddo, I think I've written about as much as I can. So what's next? I guess that's up to you. I want back in. I mean it. I know I've disappointed you as many times as a pig oinks, but kid I'm your damn mother and I ain't giving up. Not yet, not now.

I've been through hell and back. I've had one awful life and so have you. I wouldn't be surprised if you never wanted

103

to see me again. But Gus, that's not how this story is supposed to end. We've both worked too hard for it to end with us apart.

Kid, I love you. I think about you everyday. Sometimes, when I'm alone, I sit and cry and remember. Sometimes I remember the bad stuff, the abuse, and I want to vomit. But sometimes, a nice memory floats to the surface.

One time, when you were four, I took you to the amusement park. You couldn't get enough cotton candy. Then, when we got home, I caught you trying to eat real cotton. You were dipping it in mouthwash. Yecchhh!

I love you, son. You're my boy. I'll be calling Ellen next week to see where things are at. Hang in there.

Love,

Mom

8. Hello Families!

Just finished reading a letter from my mom—a long letter. It was one of those "I'm sorry, please forgive me" jobs. Screw her! After all she's put me through, the bitch expects me to welcome her back with open arms. Hell no! Not this time. Not this boy.

"Gus, you ready for dinner?"

"Go to hell! I ain't eatin' tonight."

"What did you say?"

"I said, Fuck-off, asshole...I ain't eatin' tonight!"

"Look, I don't like the food much, either. Let me close the door so we can talk about this, without everybody hearing."

"John, get the hell out of here. I just want to be alone."

"What's that?"

"A goddamn letter from my mother."

"Jesus, it goes on forever."

"That goddamn son of a bitch. Who the hell does she think she is?"

"Here, take it out on the pillow."

"I hate her! I HATE her! I HATE HER! DROP DEAD MA, YOU SON OF A BITCH. GO GET YOURSELF ANOTHER DRINK!! LEAVE ME ALONE!! LEAVE me...

....

.............................I hate crying in front of people"

John: Take this tissue and shut-up. You've got reason to scream. You've got reason to cry.

Gus: Thanks.

John: Man, your life is more up and down than

105

	a yo-yo. That really stinks.
Gus:	Hey, could we talk about this later? I just want to be alone.
John:	No problem. I'll come back later and check on you.
Gus:	Thanks.

Sometimes I just want to die. End it all. How much can a kid take before he should call it quits? I've done it before, ya know. Never wrote about it. No, not suicide. I guess it would be hard to write about that. Self-abuse. That's what I'm talking about. A few times, I've taken a razor blade and made cuts on my arm. I just couldn't take the pain *inside* anymore. The pain was like a foreign entity that lived in my innards. And there was nothing I could do about it. Life truly sucked. I couldn't get a grasp on anything. I had no control. I was being jacked around by everyone. I felt hopeless. Cutting my arms gave me some control. It let me see the pain. The old inside-out move.

I remember being self-abusive and super depressed. I think back to those periods every time my life gets turned inside out. I was lucky that I had good people around to lead me through the dark. I've learned a lot about the power of support. People need people. I've heard there's a corny song about people needing people, but it's true. I would guess most depressed, self-abusive kids feel lonely and unsupported. Even if they're living in a group home with tons of people. If you work with kids be there with them. Don't let the acting out scare you away. Every kid in a place like this is crying out for attention. Make sure they get it.

Christ, Mommie Dearest is back. God, am I ready

for this? Hey, at least I didn't put my hand through the wall. I'm doing better on the anger front. I did trash the pillow, however.

God, I really miss my mother. I try not to think about her, but she's always there. I've kind of been praying for her to come back (not that I've admitted this to anyone)...and now that she's talking about returning-I want to kill her. Can you spell A-M-B-I-V-A-L-E-N-C-E!

Ah hell, guess I'll be doing overtime with Ellen this week, El Shrinko, as I now call her.

Before I run to dinner, 'cause I am hungry, let me mention a little about the family stuff my mother was talking about. Even though I'm a little preoccupied, I think this stuff is important, and I need to think about something else right now.

The new family work seems to be making a difference. It's cool! I actually think it may result in some kids going home quicker. *(Hmm, maybe this new approach will help my mother? Stop it Gus, don't think about her.)*

On Tuesday nights, Mr. Spinelli, Vinny's grandfather, comes in and hangs out all evening. Occasionally, he cooks up a mean pizza. On Saturdays, Jack's mother and his two little sisters spend the day. Jack's mom, Rita, seemed pretty nervous when she first started coming. She hardly spoke at all. I think some of the behavior she saw really blew her away. For a while she even stopped coming. But she's been back for three or four months and seems to have loosened up a bit. She's actually a pretty good artist. She's been drawing some pictures for the kids.

At first, me and some of the other kids didn't like

the idea of parents spending time with us. For me it was like a kick in the face. At the time (and maybe even now) I had no family visiting. I was reminded of this every time a parent walked through the door.

The counselors spoke with us about this. They said some of us who don't have families visiting them might feel bad, but that it was something they had to do. They said that in time they hoped all of us would have people to visit with (i.e., new family, old family, big brother, relative, etc.).

They were right, in general. It's worked out O.K. In fact, some of the kids who don't have families really look forward to the families that do come in. Last week, however, Gordon Fletcher walked up to Hank Greeley and punched him in the face. At first, no one could figure out why. (Gordon wouldn't talk.) I knew. I wanted to punch him, too. Hank's mother had spent all afternoon cooking with us. She was really nice. Gordon and I were jealous as hell. Neither one of us even sees our mothers any more. Hank made the big mistake of having a caring mother. The bastard.

I think it must be a nice feeling for the parents to be chummin' with the staff. It looks like they're all one, big, happy family (at least most of the time).

Everyone at the Hills seems to be working together. It's wonderful.

Not only are parents constantly coming in and out of the place, but we're having some wild events, as well. On Halloween, many of the parents, Big Brothers and Sisters, staff, etc., dressed up and we had a radical party. Billy's mother came as the Executive Director. He looked good in heels. We've also had some group softball games with barbecues afterward.

The parents also have a weekly support group. I know about this because I'm sometimes recruited to help pick the parents up. At first, some of the kids were ticked. Instead of going to an activity, we were asked to round up parents. What a bore. But when it was explained, it was hard to argue about. I guess a lot of parents don't drive and/or have other kids to take care of. In the old days, according to Ellen places like the Hills would offer the groups but expect parents to make it in on their own. Wrong. A lot of them simply couldn't do it. Now, we pick up the ones who live close and some of the staff actually help watch their kids. Since the Hills started doing this, a ton more parents have gotten involved. And it's just not the driving. It's the feel. The place has become like one large community with everyone a valued member. I think the parents feel more respected.

The approach makes a lot of sense. You wonder why it took this long? Now, hey, don't think we're talking about utopia here. This changeover did cause some problems and there are still some kinks to work out. At least that's how it looks from this kid's perspective.

Christ, I overheard some of the staff really bitchin' when this whole family-centered thing was first introduced.

"Man, it's hard enough taking care of the kids! We don't need parents hanging out stirring them up."

"I'd have no idea what to say to a parent."

"Are all the kids in the family coming in? They're hellions!"

"It'll be weird consequencing a kid with his mother

there."

"What if a kid needs to be restrained? How will the parent handle that?"

These were typical comments. I think it took a lot of training before people started to feel comfortable with the idea. And, I guess, the whole thing is still evolving.

One thing they do now that blows me away concerns consequences. In the old days, if a kid screwed up the staff dealt with it. End of discussion. Finito. Now, if a kid screws up—and I'm not talking minor infraction here, I'm talking assaultive behavior, running away, stealing—you get the gist. Now, if a kid screws up, the staff get on the phone and together with the parent mete out the consequences.

Boy, the troops didn't like this wrinkle in the suit. In the old days, home and residence were usually regarded as separate. Where you screwed up is where you faced the music. Now, it doesn't matter. They're all working together. It can make you puke. It really cuts down on the fine art of "splitting" (one of our favorite pastimes).

A couple of weeks ago, two of the kids were talking about running away. The rumor spread like wild-fire. When the staff found out, they tried a new technique. Instead of talking to the two and then putting them in "close supervision," the staff called each kid's parent. Each kid spent ten minutes on the phone with his muddah. Surprise! They didn't go anywhere!

The staff say they now work as "partners" with our families. It's a gas. And it's also the reason the Hills is junking its major behavior management tool: the level

110

system. From what I understand, most group homes and residential treatment centers utilize level systems. Let me tell you a little about levels, then I'll explain why the Hills is getting rid of them.

In most level systems, kids receive points for good behavior. The points are tallied and kids are assigned a level based on how well they did. Each level allows kids certain freedoms and privileges. Earn the maximum number of points and you make the highest level, and have the most fun. Screw up and you drop levels. The low levels suck.

I think most staff members like using a level system. It helps maintain consistency and structure, and is a good feedback mechanism for the kids. Some staff members like carrying the clipboards which hold the point sheets. It's a power thing. From what I've overheard, a lot of folks are unhappy about doing away with the levels. Joan and Barbara were arguing about this last night. Joan was for 'em, Barbara against.

Joan argued that having levels reduces power battles between staff members and kids.

"We don't tell teenagers what they can and cannot do. They earn what they get. If a kid's upset with not being able to go somewhere, I tell him, 'Hey, that's the level you earned, don't blame me. Earn a higher level.' Without a level system we'll be arguing with the kids all day. I think it would be chaotic. Things generally run smoothly now. Why change things?"

(Isn't it amazing how I can remember, verbatim, what they said.)

Barbara countered:

"You're right, things do generally run smoothly. But is that our goal, to have a smooth running program?

111

Our goal is to get kids home. That's why we're making all these changes, reaching out to the families."

Does a kid's family use a level system? Hell no. If a kid is home and wants to go somewhere or do something, his mother has to decide if that's O.K. And that mother won't be checking any clipboard to see if her kid has earned the privilege, is on the right level. No, the parent will make the decision based, in general, on how her kid has been doing, and what that kid can handle.

Joan: And what if the kid doesn't like her decision and they get into a big fight?

Barbara: Then they'll have to work it out. And maybe we can help them do that. Assist them in communicating better. We can also help them by doing the same thing here. If we start dealing with the kids like their parents do, and vice-versa, hopefully, we'll all move ahead that much faster. We shouldn't be shying away from conflict. Kids will still be able to earn freedoms and privileges under the new "family-oriented" system. It just won't look and feel so artificial and regimented. It will be more humanistic. No more clipboards—just direct communicating.

Joan: I see your point. But I don't know if it will work.

Barbara: Hey, we're all a little bit nervous. But it's a step in the right direction. I read some where that there is no correlation between how well a kid is behaving at the time of discharge and post-discharge success. The only thing that seems to matter is how supported the kid and family are after discharge. Kids will feel more supported if their families use behavior practices that mirror the program's techniques.

Joan: We'll see.

At first, I was upset to hear that the level system was being abolished. It was something I could count on. I knew exactly what I could earn and I liked the constant feedback. I'm not so sure I want the staff using more discretion when it comes to what I can and can't do.

Yet, I never liked the way the staff used the level system. They frequently held it over our heads. Some seemed to get off on marking down our points and carrying around the clipboard. At times, it really felt like us versus them.

Some of the kids actually seemed obsessed about the points they were earning and the levels they were on. I never thought that was right. And lastly, some kids, the really acting-out ones, they would often stay on the lower levels forever. They never semed to earn much. In those cases, I think the system served only to reinforce the bad feelings they already harbored about themselves.

Like I said, I'm nervous about losing the level system, but I think this program is heading in the right direction. Everything they're doing seems aimed at bridging gaps and creating a supportive treatment community.

Hey, I'm not stupid. Even though I spend a lot of time looking out for Number One, I do realize what's good for us all as a whole. Having everyone communicating and working together is great. As a veteran of the social service system, and a genius to boot, I know what happens when people do their own things and communication is weak. I also know what happens when power gets misused. I know that damn well.

In a strong, equitable community, power doesn't get misused. There are too many checks and balances. Our new residential community feels better to everyone. Everyone has a voice. It's working. I'll go along with the changes.

Troubled dudes like yours truly are troubled for a reason. Usually, it's because we come from screwed up homes. Homes that were chaotic, neglectful, abusive, and inconsistent, just to name a few. So we enter the system without a clue as to what good care, good parenting is all about. Residential treatment is supposed to provide the answer. However, the answer can get muddled if profound differences continue to exist between home and treatment center. And muddle usually means acting-out. It drives us crazy when we have to choose between home and center. When programs and families really start working together, the answer grows more clear and we start to get a sense of "right" and "wrong," "good" and "bad" (i.e., we finally can make sense of the world).

What they're doing here at the Hills is putting everyone on the same page and not making assumptions about people.

Ellen, who's been a residential therapist forever

(sorry, Ellen), talked to me about this. She said when she first started, if a parent didn't come to see her at the program, the parent would often be labeled "resistant." She now realizes how wrong she (and the program) was to think this way. For the past eight months she's been doing a lot of home visits and connecting with parents she had written off. She told me she's "seen the light."

I think she's actually becoming obsessed with this whole thing. Last week while I was in her office, she got five phone calls. (You'd think the lady would have the professionalism to put her phone on "Do Not Disturb," but, NO.)

The first call was from the YMCA. Ellen's trying to get some of her families hooked in there. With a gentle push from the Hills, she's hoping she can get discounted memberships.

The second call was from St. Augustine's. Ellen was asking what kind of programs they run.

The third call was from some kind of employment development agency. Ellen wanted information about their services. Who was eligible, fees, etc.

The fourth call was from the local health clinic. She was asking whether they took Medicaid and offerred a sliding scale. She also wanted to know about sex-ed counseling.

And the fifth call was from Al's Autobody. Her car was ready.

I guess if you put two and two together you can see ol' Ellen is starting to focus bigtime on "out-of-office" therapy (as I call it). Sounds pretty good. Nice goin' El. Hey, if more families used the Y and drew more support from their local church, there'd probably be fewer kids in residential treatment.

Republicans want to build more prisons and **GET TOUGH ON CRIME!** Wow. What radical thinking. I think if you built more Y's and swimming pools, it would do more good. But who listens to a fifteen-year-old kid with zits?

Maybe I'll give my mother another chance. Who the hell knows? This new approach might help her. She's had a pretty tough life. The way they do things now is more hands-on, more supportive. I think it would reach her.

I don't think it would be easy for Ma. I can see her feeling really intimidated in the residence. No matter what she might say on the outside, on the inside she'd be questioning whether she could care for me as well as the Hills' staff. She'd watch them closely, thinking, "Can I do that?" She's always been pretty insecure. I think a lot of the parents come in like that. Can you blame them? They probably have little reason for confidence. Most have led pretty hard lives. That's what's so good about this stuff. Parents come in, feel accepted, and begin to enjoy real success with their child and the treatment staff. It's great. I'm sure most parents are used to coming in for therapy appointments where much of the focus is on what they're doing wrong. That kind of sucks.

I don't think my mother would become overbearing, but some of the mothers do. Carl's mother calls all the time. She wants to be involved in everything. I think she's burning people out. Carl wipes his ass wrong and she wants a call. With help from the staff and her program therapist, she'll probably tone down. Hey, the lady may be trying to compensate for past mistakes by getting super-involved. God bless her. Better for her to be "too" involved. I can speak to the alternative.

Thinking about my mom getting back in the picture, as well as her hanging out in my cottage, makes me very nervous. As much as I want it to happen, and yes, I do want to try (but this will be her last chance, dammit!), I wonder how she'd get along here.

Some of the kids act out a bit before their parents come in. I think some are afraid their parents won't show. Some, I think, feel their parent(s) might not fit in or prove to be embarrassing. Doug's mother had quite a mouth. And, I think there are some kids who are afraid they (the kids) won't be able to control their behavior in front of their parent(s). They may also be nervous about showing affection towards a staff member. Some of the kids have developed strong attachments to various staff members. They wonder how their parents might react to seeing these relationships. It's a lot for a kid to think about.

And then there are the kids (like 100% of us) who still struggle with feelings of anger and resentment towards their folks. These kids don't know whether to play a game with their mother or throw spaghetti in her face.

In reality, most of the kids share most of these feelings. Each one of us harbors a myriad of conflicting feelings. And they can change with the wind. Residential treatment isn't usually a short term proposition. We all need time to work through our problems and conflicts. We come to residential treatment after years of problems. There are no quick fixes.

Speaking of fixes, the Hills is doing something new

117

to make sure kids and their families do well after kids are discharged: Aftercare. Now, when a kid leaves, the kid and his family continue to receive support from the agency. They can attend groups and events at the program, will continue to meet with their program therapist, and can call the program at any time for support and/or crisis intervention. I think this makes a lot of sense.

I've been living at the Hills for a long time. When it's my turn to leave, I'll be ecstatic—but real scared. It will be weird waking up without all the structure and support places like this provide. Pretty scarey. It doesn't surprise me that a lot of kids don't make it after being discharged. I'm sure they (and maybe their families) didn't get enough support after they left. This aftercare helps with that.

A new day is dawning around here. I like it.

9. Activities, Self-Esteem &
The Globetrotters

It's 8:00 p.m. Neil, the Activities Director, is walking slowly to his car. It's been another long day. The guy works his butt off. But tonight, he won't be leaving as scheduled. Tonight, he'll be sharing an important story with you. The story of the St. Jude's Globetrotters. Although names and places will be changed, the story is true. Really.

Look, I know I'm a fictitious dude, but take my word for it, the Globetrotters were real. Everything you hear about actually happened. If you don't believe me, ask the author. He knows.

The story of the Globetrotters is a magical story about basketball, self-esteem, feeling connected, and the human spirit. The Globetrotters left an incredible legacy. To this day, their accomplishments remain an inspiration to those who knew them. They opened up eyes and changed the way certain people viewed kids in residential treatment.

I've heard the story a few times now. I love it. Afterwards, I feel as high as a kite. I guess there are quite a few messages one can draw from the story.

And that's why Neil's going to tell it.

"Yo, Neil. Stop for a second."

"What do you want, Gus? I'm really beat, can it wait until tomorrow?"

"I've got my tape-recorder primed and ready. All I need is for you to sit down at that bench, relax and tell the story."

"C'mon, I just finished five hours of softball. I'm

smelly, I'm hungry, I'm whipped. No, absolutely not, I'm not telling the story."

"But, Neil, it's for the book I'm writing. You've told me over and over to make something of my life. Well, this is what I'm doing. People should hear the story."

"Can't they hear it tomorrow?"

"Carpe diem! Live for the day! Isn't that what you preach? I'm here, man. I'm ready. Carpe diem, amigo. CARPE DIEM!"

"Ohh, why, dear Lord, did you make me such a soft touch?"

"Great. We can sit down over there, under the street light."

"Testing. One, two, three. Testing, one, two, three. Okay, all set. Ladies and gentlemen, Neil Perry and the story of the Globetrotters."

"I can't believe I'm staying here to do this."

"Just tell the story."

Tape recorder on.

It started ten years ago. At the time, I was working at a large residential treatment facility in the Northeast called St. Jude's Home. All told, there were about 90 kids living there due to various forms of abuse and/or neglect. I was the Activities Director. It was my first bigtime position. Prior to moving into that role, I served as a child care worker for two years.

The Residential Director was a big guy named Ted O'Leary. Some people had the nerve to call him "Ted," but most, like me, called him "Mr." O'Leary. A brilliant guy, he intimidated the hell out of me. Yet, he was a great boss. He knew I was a fireball of energy with a

120

modicum of talent, thus, he never stood in my way. I'd bother him all the time with new ideas and requests, and he'd never shoot me down. Sometimes, of course, he'd make it difficult. Yet I always enjoyed the interchange. It was like a game. One, in reality, we'd both win (as well as the kids).

Well, one day I walked into the mail room and checked my box. *Hmm. A letter from the Boys Club. Wonder what they want?*

YOUTH BASKETBALL LEAGUE
FRIDAY NIGHTS

LOOKING FOR NEW TEAMS
CALL: STEVE KELLY AT THE BOYS CLUB

Basketball league. Now that's a laugh. St. Jude's didn't really have a gymnasium. It had an auditorium. An old auditorium with a low ceiling and a large stage. It was a real piece of work.

Opposite the stage, maybe 90 feet across, hung one basketball hoop. The floor was a green-speckled linoleum. Hard metal screens covered the long, narrow windows that draped the sidelines. The walls were nicked-up wood panel. Pine boards with slats were used to enclose the four old-fashioned radiators that were spaced along the walls. They were painted brown. Four double doors, metal and institutional, loomed in the corners. We affectionately called this place "The Gym."

Basketball wasn't played very often at St. Jude's. That's why I laughed upon reading the notice. Besides the ceiling being too low, it was a game that the kids simply couldn't handle; no one ever wanted to pass the ball; kids would over-react to being touched; and most lacked knowledge of the game and the skills to enjoy it. As a rule, we played a lot of kickball, tag, and dodgeball. Gym trips didn't mean basketball. Basketball meant problems.

With this knowledge, I approached the nearest receptacle to dispose of the notice. As I got closer, a little spark in the brain touched off something familiar. *Wait. I thought. Our own basketball team. That would be a heck of a challenge. If I could pull it off, it would be great.*

I loved a challenge, still do.

But, *basketball? C'mon Neil, wake up. The kids fight every time they play. But what a challenge!!!*

Off I headed for the big guy's office. I needed his blessing to start the team. Of course, this would cost money. Something social service agencies don't have much of. After all, we would need uniforms and equipment. Mr. O'Leary controlled the dough.

The bum, he bought it. Gave me the green light without a whimper. *What have I got myself into this time?*

Not only was basketball a game seldom played, but I knew little about it. I was a jock, but basketball was never my game. Nevertheless, I moved ahead with it. That afternoon, I called the Boy's Club and spoke with a guy named Steve Kelly. He was in charge down there. He was really supportive of St. Jude's entering a team. He quickly sent me consent forms and promptly registered our yet unnamed team.

Some of my colleagues thought starting a team was nuts. Some thought it was a great idea. Some wondered if I could get enough kids to play without killing themselves. I wondered the same.

I sent try-out notices to all the residential units. There were six of them in the building. Twelve kids generally lived on a unit. Two of the units were for girls, the rest were for boys.

Seven kids straggled in to the try-out. Seven made it. Big surprise. Two of the kids, Pedro and Hector, 11 and 12, respectively, were great athletes. John, 11, was tall and coordinated. After that it was slim pickings. One boy, Nate, was the most hurtin' boy I had ever worked with. He tended to require a lot of physical restraining and he was not adverse to dropping a load during the process. He also liked to masturbate—a lot.

The first thing I did was have them sit on the stage and come up with a name for the team. The only one they could think of was: The Globetrotters. So we became the The St. Jude's Globetrotters. I thought it had a nice ring.

That first practice turned out to be like most of the practices: simple, loud, and tense. I didn't know any drills, and the kids were pretty anxious about putting their limited basketball skills on display. As a result, I usually had to contend with a fair amount of acting-out. The boys would pick on each other, make fart noises, and/or get in shoving matches. These guys hated to look bad in front of anyone. Each suffered with terrible self-esteem.

We were only able to schedule two practices before the first game. I had assigned each player a position (forward, guard, or center), and we had practiced the basics. As mentioned, three of the kids were good athletes and I could dribble the ball. But none of them really knew the game. To keep the practices from getting out of hand, I finished each one with a foul shooting contest. If a boy could make three foul shots in a row, he'd win a coke—to be paid later. If a kid was fooling around, he wasn't eligible to shoot. Every practice for the next six years ended this way. Later in the story, I'll talk more about the "cokes."

Prior to the first game, I went out and bought each kid a Globetrotter's shirt. They were navy blue t-shirts with red and white lettering. On the front was the Globetrotter's name, the Globe part layed out in a semi-cile. On the back, on the shoulder, was each kid's name and a large number underneath. Man, did they love those shirts. Some of the kids wanted to sleep in them.

I learned very quickly how *special* team member-ship was to these guys. Most kids who come to resi-dential treatment have never been on a team, never felt connected to anything. Those shirts came to sym-bolize a great deal. Five years later, 46 kids wanted to play for the Globetrotters—46! Mr. O'Leary, reluc-tantly, wrote the check for 46 shirts.

The day of our first game I was nervous as heck. I didn't know what to expect. I was going to take seven troubled boys into a rough part of town to engage in a game (basketball) that, previously, had been a disas-ter to play. Accompanying me would be Roger, St. Jude's gym teacher. Rog didn't know the boys very well. That also made me nervous.

All the games were played on Friday nights. That was a small blessing. In residential treatment cen-ters, school nights are often tense nights. Troubled kids worry a lot about meeting expectations. Actually, they worry most about *failing* to meet expectations. If you listen closely, a collective sigh of relief can be heard at most centers when school gets out on Friday.

As I drove my seven guys to the downtown Boy's Club, a large knot formed in my gut. *"What the hell am I doing?" I thought.*

The boys were all pretty anxious, but looked good in their t-shirts.

When you work with abused kids coming from chaotic homes, you stress structure and predictability. You make sure their living space is neat and orderly. You keep things in place. This is what makes them feel safe. When they don't feel safe they usually act-out.

Walking into the Boys Club was like walking into Penn Station at rush hour.

Whoa!!!!! There were kids everywhere. Playing pool, basketball, hanging off pipes, arguing, laughing—it was pandemonium. But it was great. This was their place. This is where they belonged.

But did *we* belong? Could my guys handle it? We'll see, I thought. We'll see. *God help me.*

Most of the kids were Hispanic. A few were black. And there seemed to be some white kids. I looked around trying to spot the people in charge. In the pool room, I noticed a tall, thin, white guy in navy sweats. He looked like he had just come in from the backwoods. He had a long, straggly beard that was more gray than black. His hair was disheveled and he wore large, thick rimmed glasses. Around his neck was the proverbial whistle. On his feet were Ked hightops.

"Hi, I'm Steve Kelly. Glad to meet you. We're psyched about St. Jude's entering a team."

Steve was an incredible guy. He was the glue that made the Boy's Club cohesive. With limited resources and a challenging group, he made that place a good place to be for the kids. In fifteen years, I've met few people I admire more.

Steve showed us around the club and helped reduce our jitters. I was pretty nervous about taking the boys into the locker room. For kids who have been sexually abused, and some of the boys had, a locker room can be one stimulating and provocative place. Fortunately, they handled it okay.

While they were getting ready, I gave them the old Knute Rockne pep talk. Win or lose I just wanted them to play hard, play clean, and have fun. I had no idea what to expect. Nate, my most troubled lad, was making a lot of weird faces and acting very silly. I kept him close.

As we walked down the corridor heading to the gym door, I saw my life pass in front of me. *What am I doing here?*

The noise was the first thing to hit us as the door opened. Whistles, screaming, chatter. It was deafening. Two games were being played simultaneouly, side by side. Each game was played on half the gym floor. The baskets were located along the sidelines. There was very little room for the players and coaches to stand. Spectators were crammed into the top two rows of a folded-up stands system. It was wall-to-wall people. *Oh, boy, how are they gonna handle this?*

Roger and I did our best to keep the boys together until our game started. But there was hardly any room to stand or sit. Finally, mercifully, a loud buzzer signalled the end of the first two games. As the teams left the court, the Globetrotters, all seven of them, trotted nervously onto the gym floor. Roger stayed with them while I checked out which court we were on. Fortunately, we had wandered onto the right court.

The team we were scheduled to play, St. Francis, hadn't arrived yet. While we waited, I had the boys practice their shooting. Balls were flying everywhere-except into the net. A few minutes passed until St. Francis appeared. Twelve well-groomed, immaculately-suited boys paraded onto the floor opposite the Globetrotters. They wore bright green tops and shorts with stylish lettering. I could see some of them pointing and laughing at our guys. I think Nate was masturbating at the time.

Before you know it, they're into this intricate lay-up drill. They were intense. They looked like a machine. I almost went in my pants. The Globetrotters looked scared. I quickly yelled to them to form their own lay-up drill. Somehow, it didn't look the same. I was in for a long night.

A loud buzzer went off and the teams were ushered to the sidelines. *Oh my God, we're actually going to play !*

I assembled the team around me and assigned positions to the starters. I reminded them it was "only a game… it doesn't matter if you win or lose…an apple a day keeps the doctor away"…I threw out every cliche I knew. We then put our hands in the middle. I yelled, "Who's gonna win?" They screamed back, "We are!" And my starters ran out to meet the Warriors of St. Francis.

It took a few minutes for Steve Kelly, who was reffing the game, to get my kids to stand in the right place. The forwards and guards had no idea where to position themselves. Finally, the whistle blew and our first game had begun.

Instant chaos. My guys, the Globetrotters, had no idea what to do out there. I'd yell to the kids to get into their positions, but they were clueless. Before I could breathe, the score was 12 - 0! I could see the substitutes on the other team laughing at us. *What have I done!*

The Globetrotters were bouncing into each other, off walls, and hacking the hell out of the other team. They weren't playing defense, they were playing "kill the guy with the ball." Kelly was doing all he could not to call every foul that was committed. Friends, it was not pretty out there. The score at halftime was 18 - 0. We rallied in the last few minutes, and they hadn't scored as much.

I gave a great pep talk during halftime. "Hey, it's our first game. Don't worry, you're all doing great. Remember, if you continue to behave well we'll stop for a snack after the game." The game was just half over but it wasn't too soon to be talking snack. I was afraid it could get ugly out there. In certain cases bribery works.

It was 24 - 0 before two unplanned events occurred. The first involved a St. Francis kid being stopped from scoring a lay-up. Unfortunately, the boy had been tripped as he ran down the sideline. I looked over and found Nate wearing a sheepish grin. "Nate! <u>Get</u> over here!" For the next two years, I never let Nate stand more than four feet away from me at any time.

The second unplanned event occurred mid-way through the fourth quarter. Pedro sunk a basket! A twenty-footer from the corner. *Thank you, God.*

I really thought we were going to be shut out. The game ended with the score, St. Francis 28 - Globetrotters 2. It was a dark day in Mudville.

In the locker room, after the game, some of my boys were pretty upset. They hated to lose. Losing and being humiliated was worse. I thought some of my boys might go after the St. Francis kids. I did what I had to do. I promised them extra snacks. It worked. I escaped from the Boy's Club without any casualties. But as I drove them to Rosie's, the local convenience store, they seemed pretty down. I tried to pick up their spirits, but, c'mon…28-2…that's bad.

Back at St. Jude's, I tried to make the game sound better than it was. I didn't tell anyone the real score. I tried to stay upbeat. But, secretly, I was worried. *Had I made a big mistake? Were these kids over their head?* I didn't sleep very well for a few nights.

Next Friday it was just as bad. We played the Holy Rosary Knights. Final score: Knights 26, Globetrotters 4. Again, the snacks bailed me out. But this was getting ugly.

I played the two games over and over in my head. Both had been living nightmares. Total chaos. The kids simply couldn't follow my directions. I'd tell a kid to play left forward and he'd go stand behind the key. On defense, they fouled like crazy.

The following Tuesday I scheduled a 5:00 p.m. practice. At 4:00 p.m., I went down to my activities office and grabbed a large roll of masking tape. I had an idea.

I got to the gym and began laying down big X's on the floor where the forwards, guards, and center should stand. I did this on both sides of the floor. When I got done, I sat alone and waited for the Globetrotters.

At five, they started coming in. "What are the X's for?" "You'll see," I explained. When they all arrived, I asked them to stand on the sideline, as if they were in a game. I then took each boy individually and showed him his position. However, I no longer called the positions forward and guard. Center remained Center.

Forward was now =   Under the Basket on This
                    Side—the near side or
                    Under the Basket on That
                    Side—the far side
Guard was now =   Away From the Basket on
                    This Side—the near side or
                    Under the Basket on That
                    Side—the far side

I told each player that whichever side he was put on is the side he stays on. If you're on "this side" on offense, you stay on "this side" for defense, no switching. You just run in a straight line from offense to defense, and vice-versa.

I then told the boys to "always keep your hands up on defense—never put them down."

We then practiced.

All they did for the next forty-five minutes was run back and forth from offense to defense, and practice being in position.

"Pedro, you're Under the Basket on this side—Go!"

"Jimmy, you're Away from the Basket on this side—Go!"

130

"Hand's up on defense! Hand's up!"

"Offense.....Defense.........Offense...Defense, Go. Go, Go!"

"John, go play Center!"

"Hector, go in for Pedro. He's Under the Basket on this side—Go!"

"Deefense, Deefense.......Hands up, Hands up!!!"

I ran their butts off. I was pleased. They seemed to get it. But, would they remember this stuff in the game. I couldn't put X's down on the Boy's Club court. For safe measure, I held another practice on Thursday and repeated the same drill. Back and forth they ran.

"Offense-Defense-Offense-Hands up!"

Hector and Pablo could run all day. They had amazing stamina. Hector had suffered lead poisoning as a kid—besides incurring his share of abuse and neglect. In addition to having incredible stamina, he was strong as an ox and a great leaper, to boot. He just wasn't very bright. I worked extra hard teaching him the X's.

Pablo was a fun kid. Dark haired and handsome, he had a wild temper but generally kept it in check. He loved the Red Sox and had a great sense of humor. He was extremely coordinated and was a promising ball handler.

John, my center, tall and blond, came from a tragic background. I'd rather not get into the specifics, but this was one hurtin' and angry kid. But he could play. And he could keep his cool.

Nick, 11, had a high I.Q. and was actually a decent athlete. He was nervous about screwing up so he, at first, never seemed to give it his all. Sometimes he got teased about his freckles.

Abner, 10, was one of my favorites. A terribly abused kid, he nevertheless had a wonderful disposition. Abner wore a crew cut and large, thick-rimmed glasses. He tended to walk in a pidgeon toed manner and wasn't very coordinated. But he tried like heck. The kid had guts.

Jerry, 10, was Abner's best friend and roommate. Jerry was everything Abner wasn't. Jerry was good looking, personable, and an okay athlete. He really looked out for Abner. I admired the two of them.

And then there was Nate, 12. This was one hurtin' kid. The most disturbed boy I had ever worked with. As the Activities Director, I spent a lot of one-to-one time with Nate. I felt bad for him. Like many of the kids, he had sufferred some serious abuse, and was now telling us about it—through his behavior. He soiled a lot and often needed to be physically restrained for long periods due to self-abusive and destructive behaviors. He came perilously close to leaving St. Jude's for a more secure treatment setting on a number of occasions.

This was my gang. It was a challenging crew. In time, I grew to love 'em.

Having lost the first game 28-2, the second 26-4, we anxiously prepared for game number three.

On game night, when I arrived at St. Jude's to pick up the boys, I was informed that Nick had tantrummed and had been brought to the "Quiet Room." Located in the basement, the Quiet Room was a place agitated kids were brought to settle down.

On each side of the room, kids sat in cubicles to relax and get focused on returning to their unit. In the two near corners of the room were isolation booths.

A tantrumming child might be brought in there to separate him from the others. The room was manned by one, sometimes two crisis workers. It could get pretty loud down there.

I went down to speak with Nick. He had tantrummed over a minor issue. Nick, like many of the kids who would play for the Globetrotters during the next six years, was scared stiff. Acting out was a way to show this and avoid the situation.

Usually, when kids are in rough shape you don't take them anywhere. You don't want them acting up more. You don't want their problems to negatively affect the others. But this was basketball, something new, something important.

I knew Nick pretty well, and felt it would be best to take him to the game even though he had just tantrummed. I figured he needed a chance to get over the hump. To see that he could succeed in such an endeavor.

It became a rather common occurrence. I'd come in early on Friday night, and go down to the Quiet Room to check which players were having pre-game jitters. Rarely would I not take a kid for behavior reasons. Once a kid went a few times, played, and did okay, the jitters (in the form of acting out) would usually go away. Playing for the Globetrotters, wearing the shirt, being part of the community, being part of the team, it was intoxicating to these guys. Most had felt like losers all their life. The Globetrotters helped change this. I slowly began to learn the incredible impact the team was having on the kids.

Okay, back to the game. After getting shellacked in the first two games, I drove the boys nervously to our third contest. *God, don't let us get embarrassed, again.*

We knew exactly where to hang our coats and change. This much was getting easier. Tonight, the opponents were the undefeated St. Augustine's Wild-cats. They wore bright yellow uniforms and knew the same fancy warm-up drills. They had one kid, I swear, as tall as Wilt Chamberlain. *Oh, boy, it's gonna be another long night!*

Before the game, while the Wildcats polished their pre-game drills, I used every minute to show my guys where the X's were. I even ran into the Wildcats zone to show the opposite X's. The Trotters seemed to un-derstand. The buzzer sounded. It was game time.

"Who's gonna win? We are!" the Globetrotters screamed prior to the tip-off. "Wilt" was jumping for the Wildcats against John. No contest. Wilt tipped it to one of his forwards and before you know it, the score was 2 - 0, Wildcats.

With a minute left in the first quarter the score was only 6 - 0, Wildcats. The Globetrotters were stay-ing in position and keeping their hands up on defense. They were playing tough! Swish!! Pedro floats one in from the top of the key. Wildcats 6, Globetrotters 2. *Hey, this ain't lookin' so bad.*

The score at halftime was 12 - 4. The final score was 18 to 8. The Globetrotters had played their butts off! The X's worked. My guys knew exactly where to play, and they were tenacious on defense.

The kids were channeling some of their angry en-ergy into the game. And it was working. Very early on, it became apparent to me that the Globetrotters was more than a basketball team. It was a chance to feel good, to succeed, to be like the "other" kids. They were hungry for this. I was hungry for this. Success breeds happiness.

Practice the next week was more upbeat. The kids knew they were improving. I continued to push the X's at them. Offense-defense-offense-defense-hands up! They were getting tighter.

Game four was against the Mt. Carmel Minutemen. They had finished second in the league last year. Prior to the game, I noticed a teacher, Mrs. Dunne, and a handful of other kids from St. Jude's in the stands. *My God, we have fans!*

"Who's gonna win? We are!" And out they went. I decided to start Nate. He hadn't received as much playing time and Mrs. Dunne was his teacher. Because he liked to masturbate, I ended up yelling "Hands up!" on both offense and defense. The other coach thought I was crazy.

The score at halftime was 14 - 8, Minutemen. Hector, John, and Pablo were playing like animals. They were everywhere! Hector was guarding a kid four inches taller, but three times in the first half he had blocked this kid's shot. Once, he sent a blocked ball screaming towards the ceiling. He was, as they say, making his presence known.

Entering the fourth quarter, the Minutemen led 22 - 14. No one scored for a few minutes, and then John got hot. Boiling hot! He started sinking everything he threw up. Meanwhile, Hector had taken over on defense. He was swatting balls away like flies. With 40 seconds to go, the Minutemen led by 2, 26-24. My heart was pumpin' out of my chest. I was screamin' at the top of my lungs for the guys to get in position

135

and keep their hands up. Our fans were chanting: "Trotters, Trotters, Trotters!" It was wild. With twenty seconds to go, Pedro steals the ball and sinks a lay-up! Tie score! Tie score! 26 - 26!

The Minutemen inbound the ball. Number 7, their tallest player catches it and drives for a lay-up. Out of nowhere, Hector flies in and rejects the ball. Nick picks it up and passes to Pablo. Pablo dribbles down the right side and launches a bomb with four seconds remaining. The ball goes in and out. Between two Minutemen defenders, John leaps for the rebound. He grabs it and lets a shot go just as the final buzzer sounds. *SWISH!!! GLOBETROTTERS WIN!!!! 28-26!*

It was the '67 Red Sox all over again! There was pandemonium on the court. The kids were grabbing each other. The fans were pounding us all on the backs. We were delirious!! To this day, I rank that moment as truly one of the great moments of my life. I'll never forget it.

I took the entire team out for sundaes. We had a blast. We marched back into St. Jude's chanting: "We're number one...We're number one"...it was great. That night I made up a huge banner describing the game and hung it in the front lobby. I would hang a banner after each game for the next six years. I wanted these guys to remember their successes. I wanted the world to know these guys could make it.

As the successes mounted, more kids wanted to play. No kid was turned down. They each got a shirt. I would take ten boys to a game. Every Thursday I'd post that week's participants.

At the end of the first season, our record was 3 wins and 11 losses. It had been a successful year. By the conclusion of the season, 14 kids had joined the team. Each proudly wore the Globetrotter shirt with his name on the back.

To trumpet the success, we held an award's banquet. During the season, I had taken slides of the team. At the banquet, which the kids needed to dress up for, we had a fancy dinner in the gym, catered by the child care staff. After dinner, we watched the slides, and then handed out trophies. I tried to make the trophy presentations as dramatic as possible.

The banquet became an annual event. (I'd have to wheel and deal with Mr. O'Leary every year in order to get top class trophies, but after some good natured jousting, he'd always give in.)

Every year for six years we fielded a team. The Globetrotters became an institution. In year four, we made the play-offs and finished second overall. The semi-final game was played in front of a packed audience. Over a hundred parents, staff, and kids showed up to root us on. We won that game in the last three seconds when Mike Youngbird sank a bomb from 10 feet inside the half-court line. I remember screaming at him to pass the ball!

In year five, 46 kids tried out for the team. Mr. O'Leary let me buy 46 shirts. I had to break them into 3 practice squads.

Needless to say, when it comes to the Globetrotters I have a lot of fond memories. But, more importantly, I learned a great deal from those gutsy performers.

I learned how important it is for troubled kids to "fit in." How desperately they want to feel "connected." And I learned how far they'd go to achieve these feelings.

I saw kids who would tantrum at St. Jude's if a kid just looked at them the wrong way, get pushed, bumped, tripped, and teased during a game—without any retalliation whatsoever.

They all knew that if they acted up during a game, they wouldn't play again for awhile. In six years of games, I never had a serious behavior problem. <u>Not one</u>. And I often took some of our most acting out, disturbed kids!

Abused and neglected kids feel like losers. If you work with such kids do your best to make them feel like winners. Years after the first Globetrotter took the floor, ex-players would return to visit St. Jude's. "I still have my trophy," I'd hear over and over. And the Globetrotter shirts would be worn until the kids literally busted through them. Some would sleep in them.

When a kid does something good, trumpet it. I still remember the kids showing their teachers and parents the banner with their name on it: "Billy Hopkins plays great defense!" "Tommy Mackenty scores six big points!" If a kid played he got his name on that week's banner.

My whole orientation to working with troubled kids changed as a result of the Globetrotter experience. I know there's a lot of psychological hocus-pocus out there, but for me, in my work, it all comes down to self-esteem building. The Globetrotters demonstrated how far a kid could travel if he began to believe in himself. And if he felt *you* believed in him.

In retrospect, the secret of the Globetrotters success lay in its universal opportunity for individual success. Any kid who wanted to play made the team, got a shirt, played, made the banner, and received a trophy. In the business, they call such tangible reminders transitional objects. Years later, that trophy sitting on a kid's bureau reminds him of a prior success. Transitional objects can warm and energize a struggling soul.

Modifying the rules of the game also helped. This was an important factor in our success. I've carried this lesson with me. Remember, Gus, in chapter one, you spoke about me not allowing kids to strike out in softball. "It's always spring training." That's a carry-over rule from my Globetrotter days.

If kids aren't afraid to strike out more will want to play. And will grow from the experience. If basketball terminology is easier to understand, more kids will come and enjoy it.

Kids with low self-esteem shy away from activities they think will cause them embarrassment. Better safe than sorry. Being a Globetrotter was safe. A softball game in which you can't strike out is safe. Get the point, amigo?

Sometimes, Gus, I'll be driving home at night or lying in bed and my mind will take me back to the St. Jude's gym. And I'll remember the kids busting through the doors, with their navy blue Globetrotter shirts, ready to practice.

Or, I'll see Pablo running up to me, all bubbly and excited, wanting to talk about our last game. I'll see Hector jumping three feet in the air to block a shot. I'll remember returning to St. Jude's after our first win like conquering heroes, chanting: "We're number one, we're number one..."

And I'll never forget Chris Nipper walking up to receive his trophy. The kid had four leg operations but played his heart out. A lot of tears fell when Chris walked down that aisle.

Being a Globetrotter meant a lot to the kids, but it meant even more to me. Sometimes, in this business, we're taught not to expect too much from the children. They come to us with labels and histories that, frankly, make us wonder about their futures. On a daily basis, we experience and try to manage very difficult behavior. Put it all together and even the best of us, occasionally, loses hope. Many of us burn-out. It becomes too much. The spark inside us that burned brightly when we first started, dims or is extinguished.

For fifteen years my spark has burned brightly. I have my bad days. I have my bad weeks. Heck, 1990, wasn't much fun. But, as they say in Star Wars epics, "May the force be with you."

The force has remained strong in me. I think, in large part, because of my friends, the Globetrotters. May the force be with them.

Gus: Thanks, Neil. I love that story.
Neil: No, thank you. It was good to remember.
Gus: So what about the cokes?
Neil: Oh, yea, the cokes, the kids could earn
         by shooting 3 foul shots in a row at the
         end of practice.
Gus: You said you'd talk more about them.
Neil: At the end of the first year, during the
         banquet, Nick brought a note to me
         signed by all the players. It read:

Dear Coach,

Thanks for coaching the team. You don't have to pay us the cokes.
                    The Globetrotters

Each kid had signed it. The note became an annual tradition. I loved those guys.

10. Final Thoughts

This is it, the final chapter. I don't have a whole lot more to say. I don't have any more guts to spill. Ol' Gus is ready to call it a day.

I'm seeing my mother tomorrow. I can't think about anything else. I haven't slept since I got her letter. I'm a wreck. Maybe this time it will be different. Who the hell knows? I do like the way this place is now working with families. And, I still love my mother. So what the heck, I'll give it one more try. God, please, let it work this time!

Writing this book has been fun. It's also been painful. I didn't, as they say, leave many stones unturned. But, no pain—no gain. (You got to love cliches.)

I wrote this book to help people better understand kids. We're not that complicated. We all want to be loved and cared for. When that doesn't happen, we react negatively. Big surprise.

Acting-out behavior is nothing more than a message to the world that something isn't right. Kids don't act out because they're feeling good. They act out to get things changed.

Sure, kids need to be consequenced for screwing up. But not at the expense of the reason why. I can't stress this enough.

I don't believe there is an entity called a "bad" kid. There are only kids who act "bad" because they've had "bad" luck. That's it in a nutshell. Believe me.

Kids like me, hard-luck kids, grow up believing we're bad. Teachers yell at us. Police yell at us. Parents yell at us. It's an easy pill to swallow. Somewhere along the line, the record needs to be set straight.

That's what good residential treatment, foster care, and counseling can do (if a troubled kid and his family are lucky enough to receive such help).

I'm just starting to believe that the abuse and neglect I suffered wasn't my fault. Luckily, I have some damn good people helping me.

Damn good people. Let me take some time to thank them. And to thank all of you who work with children and their families. As Gomer Pyle would say: "Thank You, Thank You, Thank You!"

You don't get paid much. You take a lot of bull. And you never seem to receive the recognition you deserve. But you keep coming back, day after day, month after month, year after year. And some of you, a lot of you, truly make a difference. I don't know where I'd be today without the Neils, Ellens, and Margarets who have been there for me. Words can't adequately express the love and gratitude I feel towards these people. And all such people who give of themselves to help others.

We only go around once in this world. Kids only get one chance at being kids. Help us grow. Help us live. We're worth it!

About the Author

Charlie Appelstein, M.S.W., President of Appelstein Professional Services, provides training, consultation, and literature to psychiatric, residential, foster care, and educational settings throughout the U.S. and Canada. From 1987 to 1993, he served as the Residential Director and Treatment Coordinator for the Nashua Children's Home, a mid-sized residential facility for at-risk kids and their families. In 1991, Charlie won first place honors in the bi-annual Albert E. Trieschman Child Care Literature Competition—essay category, for a paper which has subsequently become *The Gus Chronicles*. His second book, *No Such Thing As a Bad Kid: Understanding and Responding to the Challenging Behavior of Troubled Children and Youth* was published in 1998.

Charlie and his wife and daughter reside in southern New Hampshire. He can be contacted at his business office:

Appelstein Professional Services
12 Martin Ave. Office B
Salem, New Hampshire 03079

charliea@attbi.com
Website: www.charliea.com

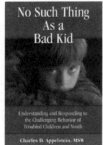

No Such Thing As a Bad Kid

Understanding and Responding to the Challenging Behavior of Troubled Children and Youth

Charlie Appelstein, M.S.W.

Written specifically for teachers, child and youth-care professionals, and foster parents, *No Such Thing As a Bad Kid* is packed with information for *anyone* who lives or works with youngsters at risk. This empowering handbook provides hundreds of hands-on tips and sample dialogues which can help revolutionize your interactions with troubled kids and their interactions with the world. Even parents of children *not* at risk will benefit from this book.

"Anyone concerned with troubled and at-risk youth will be captured by this treasure of practical strategies for respectful behavior management. It is a refreshing new resource."
– Larry Brendtro
President
Reclaiming Children and Youth

"A timely and significant new book that will truly help teachers – at all levels – to better understand and engage their most challenging students."
– Michelle Booth, Former Executive Director
Project Alliance, Massachusetts

"Sure to be an instant classic."
– Dennis Braziel, MSSA, LSW
Senior Consultant, Child Welfare League of America

About the Publisher

The Gifford School is a private, nonprofit day school with over thirty years of experience providing quality educational and clinical services to students with special academic, behavior, and emotional needs.